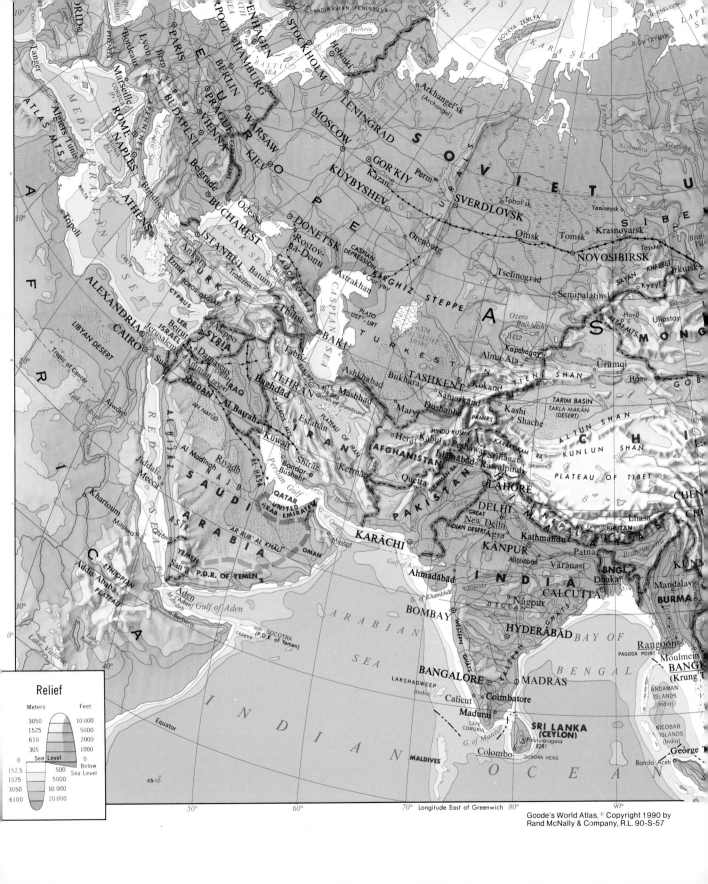

SCANDINAVIAN PENINSULA

NOVAYA ZEMLYA

KARA SEA

LAPTEV SEA

P. OV TAYMYR

MYS CHELYUSKIN

COPENHAGEN

STOCKHOLM

Gulf of Bothnia

Helsinki

Arkhangel'sk
(Archangel)

HAMBURG

BALTIC SEA

LENINGRAD

MOSCOW

GOR'KIY

Perm

Tobol'sk

Yeniseysk

SIBE

BERLIN

WARSAW

KIEV

KUYBYSHEV

Ryazan'

SVERDLOVSK

Omsk

Tomsk

Krasnoyarsk

PRAGUE

VIENNA

BUDAPEST

E U R O P E

Kazan'

SVERDLOVSK

Orenburg

Tselinograd

NOVOSIBIRSK

Tayshet

Irkutsk

BUCHAREST

Odessa

DONETSK

Rostov-
na-Donu

CASPIAN
DEPRESSION

KIRGHIZ

Gur'yev

STEPPE

A

Semipalatinsk

SAYAN KHREBET

Hovd

Kyzyl

ALTAI MTS.

MONG

ATHENS

ISTANBUL

Ankara

Izmir

T U R K E Y

Trabzon

Batumi

Tbilisi

CAUCASUS MTS.

Astrakhan

PLATO
UST'-URT

Ozero
Balkhash

1112

Uliastay

GOB

ROME

NAPLES

BELGRADE

Black Sea

TOROS DAGLARI

Tabriz

BAKU

CASPIAN
SEA

T U R K E S T A N

Alma-Ata

Kapchagay

TIEN SHAN

Ürümqi

Hami

CYPRUS

LEB.

Beirut

ISRAEL

Jerusalem

Aleppo

SYRIA

Damascus

TEHRAN

MTS. Mashhad
Qolleh-ye Damávand

Ashkhabad

Bukhara

Samarkand

Dushanbe

PAMIRS

Kashi

Shache

TARIM BASIN
TAKLA MAKAN
(DESERT)

ALTUN SHAN

CAIRO

ALEXANDRIA

LIBYAN DESERT

JORDAN

Amman

IRAQ

Baghdad

Eşfahān

Qom

I R A N

ZAGROS MTS.

Marv

Herat

Kabul

HINDU KUSH

Peshawar Srinagar

KARAKORAM RA.

Islāmābād Rawalpindi

KUNLUN SHAN

PLATEAU OF TIBET

Tropic of Cancer

Suez

Al Başrah

Kuwait

Bandar-e
Büshehr

Shiraz

Kerman

AFGHANISTAN

Quetta

LAHORE

Lhasa

Aswán

AR NAFUD

Al Madinah

Riyadh

NAJD

Persian Gulf

QATAR

UNITED
ARAB EMIRATES

PAKISTAN

DELHI

New Delhi

GREAT
INDIAN DESERT

Āgra

Everest

Kathmandu

BHUTAN

Patna

Lhasa

CHEN

CHO

CHI

RED SEA

Jiddah

Mecca

SAUDI

ARABIA

AR RUB' AL KHALI

OMAN

Muscat

KARĀCHI

Ahmadābād

KĀNPUR

Allāhābād

Vārānasi

Patna

BNGL.

Dhaka

KUNM

Khartoum

Milswa

Qizan

ASIR

YEMEN

San'a

P.D.R. OF YEMEN

Gulf of Kutch

I N D I A

Nāgpur

DECCAN

CALCUTTA

Mandalay

BURMA

ETHIOPIAN
PLATEAU

Addis Ababa

Aden
(Adan) Gulf of Aden

Moldera

SOCOTRA
(P.D.R. of Yemen)

Berbera

A R A B I A N

S E A

BOMBAY

HYDERĀBĀD

WESTERN GHATS

EASTERN GHATS

BAY OF

BENGAL

Rangoon

PAGODA POINT

Moulmein

BANGK

(Krung

Lake Victoria

Lake
Rudolf

Equator

BANGALORE

LAKSHADWEEP
(India)

Calicut

Coimbatore

Madurai

MADRAS

ANDAMAN
ISLANDS
(India)

NICOBAR
ISLANDS
(India)

George

CAPE
COMORIN

G. of Mannar

SRI LANKA
(CEYLON)

Piduru talagala
8281

DONDRA HEAD

Colombo

MALDIVES

I N D I A N     O C E A N

45-12

## Relief

| Meters | | Feet |
|---|---|---|
| 3050 | | 10 000 |
| 1525 | | 5000 |
| 610 | | 2000 |
| 305 | | 1000 |
| 0 | Sea Level | 0 |
| | | Below |
| | | Sea Level |
| 152.5 | | 500 |
| 1525 | | 5000 |
| 3050 | | 10 000 |
| 6100 | | 20 000 |

50°     60°     70° Longitude East of Greenwich 80°     90°

*Enchantment of the World*

# IRAQ

*By Leila Merrell Foster*

---

**Consultant for Iraq:** Louay Bahry, Ph.D., author; former Professor of Political Science, University of Baghdad, Baghdad, Iraq

**Consultant for Reading:** Robert L. Hillerich, Ph.D., Bowling Green State University, Bowling Green, Ohio

**CHILDRENS PRESS®**
CHICAGO

*The Shiite shrine in Karbala is the destination of Shiite pilgrims.*

**Where several English spellings of Arabic names exist, Childrens Press has used a modified version of the transliteration system used by the Library of Congress.**

Library of Congress Cataloging-in-Publication Data

Foster, Leila Merrell.
  Iraq / by Leila M. Foster.
    p.    cm. — (Enchantment of the world)
  Includes index.
  Summary: Discusses the geography, history, people, and culture of this strategically located Middle Eastern country.
  ISBN 0-516-02723-9
  1.  Iraq—Juvenile literature.  [1.  Iraq.]  I.  Title.
II.  Series.
DS70.6.F67  1990                   90-2174
956.7—dc20                         CIP
                                 AC

Second printing, 1992.

**Picture Acknowledgments**
**AP/Wide World Photos:** 64, 65, 67 (left), 68 (right), 70 (2 photos), 73, 77
**The Bettmann Archive:** 41, 52, 62 (2 photos), 67 (right), 68 (left), 71 (2 photos), 72, 82, 92, 107 (left)
© **Virginia Grimes:** © Oriental Institute, 23 (right), 34
**Historical Pictures Service, Chicago:** 23 (left), 31, 58, 59, 61 (2 photos), 81
**North Wind Picture Archives:** 48 (2 photos), 55
**Oriental Institute:** 21, 25 (right), 29, 42 (center & right), 45 (left), 46 (2 photos)
**Photri:** 4, 5, 10, 47 (left), 50, 83 (left), 85 (bottom left), 100 (bottom left), 103, 104, 106 (2 photos), 107 (right); © **Nik Wheeler,** 16 (center & right), 83 (right), 84 (left & center), 85 (bottom right), 88 (center & right), 100 (bottom right), 102 (center left & bottom right), 109 (bottom), 112 (left), 113 (center & right); © **Fovea,** 16 (left), 84 (right), 100 (top)
**H. Armstrong Roberts:** 80
**Root Resources:** © Robert Biggs, 86 (right), 94 (bottom right)
**SuperStock International, Inc.:** 9 (right), 79, 85 (top left & right), 94 (left), 108 (right), 111; © **Peter Schmid,** 6, 47 (right), 86 (left), 87, 88 (left), 90, 94 (top right), 95, 96, 102 (top right); © **Kurt Scholz,** Cover, Cover Inset, 12, 25 (left), 27, 39, 45 (right), 56, 97, 109 (top), 110 (2 photos); © **Silvio Fiore,** 42 (left); © **George Ricotto,** 74, 102 (top left), 102 (bottom left); © **N.C. Valentine,** 98, 112 (right), 113 (left)
**Len W. Meents:** Maps on 7
**Maps:** 1, 2, 101, 105, 108 (left), 111 (right), 114
**Courtesy Flag Research Center, Winchester, Massachusetts 01890:** Flag on back cover, 9 (left)
**Cover: Iman Abba Mosque in Karbala**
**Cover Inset: Human headed bull—Assyrian Nimrud**

*Handwoven carpets cover the ground in a tent where tea is served to guests.*

## TABLE OF CONTENTS

*Burning off natural gas at an oil refinery in Kirkuk.*

# Chapter 1

# THE LAND
# BETWEEN TWO RIVERS

Iraq is a nation with enormous economic and political potential. Its oil resources are among the largest in the world. It has a sufficiently large population and water supply to develop other industries in its economy. Its strategic location at the eastern edge of Arab countries, close to the Soviet Union, and a barrier to the regional ambitions of Iran make it an important player in international politics.

The territory of Iraq is where much of civilization began. It has been the capital of many great empires that extended their power throughout the Fertile Crescent. The Fertile Crescent is the territory that is roughly shaped like a crescent and follows the population settlements between the Tigris and Euphrates rivers over to the Mediterranean Sea and down the Nile River valley. It was the site of important trade routes between the Eastern and Western worlds.

The ancient name for the territory of Iraq is *Mesopotamia,* which means "the land between the two rivers"—the Tigris and the Euphrates. The modern name, Iraq, is the Arabic word for cliff— one of the geographic features of the country.

The national flag has three equal horizontal stripes of red, white, and black. On the middle white stripe are three, five-pointed green stars. The flag was adopted in 1963. The national emblem is an eagle adapted from the standard carried by Saladin, a Muslim hero during the Crusades in the eleventh to the thirteenth centuries. Against the eagle is the shield that is like the flag, although vertical instead of horizontal. The Arabic script at the bottom says "Republic of Iraq."

## BOUNDARIES

Iraq is a little larger than the state of California or the South American country of Paraguay. Its area is 169,235 square miles (438,317 square kilometers). That figure includes 357 square miles (925 square kilometers) of territorial inland water and the Neutral Zone south of Iraq. The diamond-shaped Neutral Zone lies between Iraq and Saudi Arabia. Since 1920 this zone was administered jointly by the two countries. But a 1975 agreement that was initialed, but not ratified, evenly divided the area between the two countries.

On the east, Iraq shares a boundary with Iran; on the north, with Turkey; on the northwest, with Syria; on the southwest, with Jordan and Saudi Arabia; and on the south, with Saudi Arabia, Kuwait, and the waters of the Persian, or Arabian, Gulf. The dispute over the border with Iran was one of the reasons for the recent long war with that country. The inclusion of the northern province with Mosul in Iraq and its rich oil deposits was decided as recently as 1926. Both Turkey and Syria claimed the area. Also in the north are people called the Kurds who hope to have their own nation.

*Above: Iraq's flag   Right: A group of camels in the desert*

## GEOGRAPHICAL ZONES IN THE COUNTRY

Iraq has four main geographical divisions: desert in the west and southwest, dry rolling grasslands between the upper Tigris and Euphrates rivers, highlands in the north and east, and a low plain through which the lower Tigris and Euphrates flow.

The desert stretches west and south of the Euphrates River. It is part of a larger desert area that extends into Syria, Jordan, and Saudi Arabia. Few people live in this stony plain that has some sandy areas. This zone is lined with wadis, watercourses that are dry most of the year. However, during the winter season, rain can fill these wadis with dangerous torrents of water. Some of the watercourses are 200 miles (322 kilometers) long.

The rolling upland area between the Tigris River north of Samarra and the Euphrates north of Hit, is sometimes called Al-Jazirah (the island). The water in this landscape has cut deep valleys. Irrigation of crops is difficult here, but there is some rain-fed agriculture.

*The highlands of Iraq*

The highlands begin just southwest of Mosul and Kirkuk. They extend to the borders with Iran to form the northeast zone. Foothills and steppe change to mountains ranging from 3,000 to 12,000 feet (913 to 3,658 meters) near the borders of Iran and Turkey. The mountain area has several valleys suitable for agriculture. However, in the foothills and steppe, the soil and rainfall can support crops. Kirkuk, the center of the region, is where some of the great oil fields are located.

The low plain of Baghdad begins north of Baghdad, Iraq's

capital, and extends to the gulf. Most of the population lives in or near this plain. It is called an alluvial plain because it is built up by the mud and sediment laid down by the river systems. In many places the Tigris and Euphrates rivers are above the level of the plain—just as is true of the Mississippi River down in Louisiana in the southern United States. This 45,000 square mile (116,550 square kilometer) area is the delta, or end point, of the rivers that flow into the gulf. The territory is grooved by river channels and irrigation canals. When the rivers flood, lakes are formed. A large area (about 6,000 square miles; 15,540 square kilometers) is marshland that extends into Iran. It has been estimated that the silt that is carried by the river and the irrigation canals and the silt that is carried by the wind build up the delta plains at the rate of 8 inches (20 centimeters) a century. Big floods can result in a deposit of as much as 12 inches (30 centimeters) of mud in some of the temporary lakes. Unfortunately the rivers also carry large quantities of salts that are bad for the crops. Because of the high water table and poor drainage, the unwanted salts are concentrated near the surface. Farming productivity in the region south of al-Amarah is limited because of this problem with the soil.

## THE RIVERS

The two great rivers of Iraq are the Tigris and the Euphrates. The water of these rivers is an important resource of the country today. It undoubtedly made the beginning of civilization possible here. People were able to settle in cities and take advantage of cultivation of food plants and easy transportation on the water.

The Tigris begins in Turkey and is 1,150 miles

*The Tigris River (above) winds through Iraq before it joins with the Euphrates River to form the Shatt al-Arab River.*

(1,851 kilometers) long. The Euphrates, which is 1,460 miles (2,350 kilometers) long, also begins in Turkey, then flows into Syria, and on into Iraq. The Tigris and the Euphrates meet in southern Iraq at al-Qurnah to form the river known as the Shatt al-Arab, which flows 115 miles (185 kilometers) into the gulf. It is this waterway that has been involved in the disputed boundary with Iran. The Tigris is narrower than the Euphrates, but carries more water. North of the city of Baghdad, the Tigris and Euphrates have valley walls that keep them in well-defined channels. Below the capital, the rivers meander, and have frequently changed course, leaving behind abandoned riverbeds. In this flat land, the spring floods can spread out over a considerable territory. Moreover, since the Tigris can rise at the rate of 1 foot (.3 meters) per hour, flooding can be sudden. Flood control and irrigation systems are helping to prevent some of the destruction experienced in the past.

The rivers in many ways have been water highways over the centuries. Yet the rivers also create problems for good transportation. Flooding in the lower sections make roadbuilding difficult. In the upper regions of the rivers, boats can only travel downstream because of the fast current. Near the gulf, the rivers are wide and slow, but often very shallow. Dredging is necessary to allow shipping.

## CLIMATE

Iraq has two seasons. During the six months from November through April, 90 percent of the rainfall occurs. Most of this rain falls during the winter, from December to March. The dry season is from May to October. June, July, and August are very hot.

The mean annual rainfall is between 4 and 7 inches (10 and 17 centimeters) in most of the country, except in the north and northeast. In the mountains, rain is more plentiful, reaching 40 inches (102 centimeters) a year in some spots. However, because of the rugged terrain there, the rain is not very useful for cultivation of crops. Only in the valleys, foothills, and steppe, where 12 inches (30 centimeters) or more of rain may fall annually, is cultivation possible without irrigation. However, even here shortage of rain can lead to crop failure. Only one crop a year can be grown.

Rain can be a problem as well as a gift to a desert area. Five or six days of steady rain can turn roads into thick mud and disrupt postal and telephone communication. Planted crops can be washed out. Houses and roofs made of mud can leak badly. Fortunately most buildings can be repaired when the rain stops.

Winter temperatures range from below freezing in the north and northeastern foothills and the western deserts to the upper 30 degrees Fahrenheit (3.3 degrees Celsius) in the alluvial plains of the south. The high readings at this time of year are from 55 to the lower 60 degrees Fahrenheit (12.7 to 17.2 degrees Celsius). Summer temperatures range from the lower 70s to 110 degrees Fahrenheit (22.7 to 43.4 degrees Celsius). Extreme temperature in the western desert go from 6 degrees to over 115 degrees Fahrenheit (-14 degrees to 46 degrees Celsius).

Around the rivers and irrigation canals, the humidity adds to the discomfort felt from the heat. In Baghdad, the city comes alive in the summer after 6:00 P.M. when it is cool enough to enjoy the markets, the parks, and the restaurants. In the country in the summer, the cool of the night also is the time for activity and visiting. The heat of the day is good only for sleeping and saving one's energy. It is no wonder that cooler underground rooms or courtyards with a breeze are favored for sleeping.

Two types of wind are famous in Iraq. A dry dusty wind from the south or southeast is called a *sharqi*. It can gust up to fifty miles (eighty kilometers) an hour, carrying with it dust that rises up to several thousand feet, often closing down airports. These storms usually come at the change of seasons. In mid-June to mid-September, the prevailing wind from the north and northwest is called the *shamal*. It is a very dry air that permits the sun to heat up the land, though the breeze does help to cool it a little.

The shortage of rain and the extreme heat are what make much of Iraq desert. Soil and plants lose the moisture they do get from the rain very quickly through evaporation.

## THE PEOPLE

The population, approximately seventeen million people, is sufficient to provide the labor needed for industrial growth. However, the ratio of people to land is low enough that the country can support the increase that may be expected when infant mortality rates are reduced with better health care. Most of the population live in cities and towns with many people from rural areas moving to urban centers to seek better wages.

The official language of Iraq is Arabic. An estimate of the languages spoken is: Arabic, 79 percent; Kurdish, 16 percent; Persian, 3 percent; and Turkish, 2 percent.

Islam is the national religion, and 95 percent of the population are Muslims. Two major Islamic groups live in Iraq: Shiites and Sunnis. While more than 50 percent are Shiites, the leaders of the party in power since 1968 are mostly Sunnis. There is a very small Jewish population, some of whom date their families to the Babylonian Exile (586-516 B.C.). Most of the Jews have left Iraq because of negative attitudes toward the formation of the Israeli state. There are a number of Christian communities that are related to different denominations and represent descendants of persons who did not convert to Islam when that religion was introduced.

The people have many different life-styles. In the extreme south of the country, in the delta area of the marshes, there are Arabs who spend most of their lives in boats and rafts fishing and

*Left to Right: A camel herder in the desert, a Kurdish mother and child, and marsh Arabs, the people who live in the southern delta area of the marshes*

hunting birds and wild animals. The nomads in western Iraq are like those of Saudi Arabia, Syria, and Jordan who follow their flocks to good pastures. From Baghdad north, along the great caravan routes, there is a greater mix of people. Baghdad, itself, has had a recent influx of Egyptians and Palestinians. It is a sophisticated cosmopolitan center of government, education, and the arts. In the far north, in the hill country and mountain region, live the most significant minority, the Kurds. Although they are Sunni Muslims, the Kurds have their own culture and language. They have a sense of national identity with the Kurds who live in the countries that border their territory.

16

# Chapter 2

# CIVILIZATION'S

# BEGINNINGS

---

Many important civilizations have lived in Iraq. Sumerians, Akkadians, Babylonians, Assyrians, Persians, Greeks, Romans, Arabs, Mongols, and Turks—all have called this country home and have contributed to modern Iraq. The history of humans can be traced far back in time to discover how people lived in these great civilizations.

## BEFORE WRITTEN HISTORY

Even without written records, which were developed very early in this country, archaeologists are able to tell us how people lived by examining artifacts and other things left behind. The earliest items are hand axes and scrapers that date back to 120,000 B.C. found in the northern part of Iraq. Some of these finds were at campsites or workshops that later were covered over; some were found in caves.

In the Shanidar Cave, scientists found bones of oxen, sheep, and goats. That suggests there was a moderately cold climate. They also discovered some tortoise shells and nine human skeletons. The skull of one skeleton was restored to reveal a Neanderthal man about thirty-five years old. A scientist looking at these skeletons could tell that one of the men had an arm amputated with a flint knife. Some of the people were killed by blocks falling from the roof of the cave. Other skeletons were discovered at a lower level in the cave. The scientists have dated three that were discovered higher in the cave as living about forty-five thousand years ago, while the ones found lower could be as old as sixty thousand years.

About nine thousand years ago a great change took place in northern Iraq and in other parts of the Near East. Humans tamed and domesticated animals. They learned how to plant crops rather than just gather them. Humans settled in one place and built houses out of clay, which was plentiful. Metal began to be used in place of the limited supply of stone. Several families lived together and they figured out how to govern themselves. Villages grew to the size of cities. Cities formed kingdoms and eventually the kingdoms became empires.

## SUMERIAN CIVILIZATION

Sometime between 3500 and 3000 B.C., a group of people called the Sumerians gathered together in cities along the rivers in southern Iraq. They formed the city-states in which civilization developed with many inventions that we now take for granted — for example, the wheel, writing, and counting.

Perhaps the climate became drier than it had been, making the water of the rivers even more valuable. The rivers washed down silt, creating soil that was good for crops. With the spring floods, the soil was enriched each year. At first, the farmers may have simply carried the water to their fields to keep their plants alive in the hot summers. Then, they may have permitted breaks in the natural levees or dams that form along the riverbank and channeled the water into ditches. They built dams to collect some of the water away from the river. This water could be bailed out later and used on the fields.

When the Sumerians saw how well this system worked, they dug canals that carried the water to fields several miles from the river. They developed plows, perhaps at first a crooked tree or branch but later made out of bronze. They began to use their oxen to pull the plow. They even developed a planter by attaching a funnel to the plow for seeds. This efficiency in agriculture was important to the development of civilization, because it freed some persons for work other than the production of food.

The Sumerians needed to measure slopes and flow patterns in the water ditches of their irrigation system. They developed instruments for measurement and calculation and the mathematics to make these useful.

Since metals were not found in this territory, trade was necessary with the mountain areas to obtain the raw materials for the bronze.

Planting and harvesting is done best with some kind of calendar. The Sumerians developed a calendar that is based on lunar months of twenty-eight days. Six thousand years ago they observed the heavens and recorded unusual events, like the sudden appearance of a bright star that we would call a supernova. Our astronomers confirm the presence of such an event then by their observations of the condition of the star now.

Wheels were invented. At first these were solid, without any spokes. The wheel also was used as the disc that potters rotate in order to shape a round pot. Wheels on carts and sails on boats meant that goods and supplies could be moved farther faster.

If speculations about a climate change are correct, then as the land became drier, the territory along the rivers became more important for crops. People began to move out of the dry zones and cluster in the cities that sprang up along the rivers.

The Sumerians asked themselves why they had good crops in some years, but were washed out or lacked enough water at other times. They believed that some three thousand gods and goddesses controlled all of life and nature. The four main deities governed heaven, air, earth, and water. Humans were thought to have been formed by the gods out of clay in order to serve as their slaves. The Sumerian gods and goddesses were very much like humans in eating, drinking, getting married, and fighting. They let humans know what they wanted by communicating with the priests and priestesses through omens. If the liver of a sheep sacrificed to a god was of a particular shape, this was an omen that might mean that the god needed more grain or beer. The Sumerians were anxious and pessimistic about their lives that were filled with uncertainty about crops, disease, and wars. They did their best to appease their deities with offerings and prayers in order to ward off calamities.

Religion was important to the Sumerians, and the temples to their gods became their most important buildings. Using the same mud bricks that were the building materials of their homes, the Sumerians created temples on platforms. Eventually, as the city-states grew and as the mud buildings required rebuilding after the rains, the structures were constructed higher with steps up to the sanctuary at the top. These buildings are called ziggurats.

As the temples grew in size and influence, they created the need for specialized jobs—spiritual leaders, administrators, conductors of ceremonies, artists, musicians, cooks, weavers, and

*A cylinder seal (left) and the impression created when the seal is used (right). Two gods are shown: one is using a plow and the other has a left hand shaped like a scorpion. A crescent, a star, and a bird are in the background.*

fieldworkers. These people, together with widows and orphans who were cared for by the temples, had to be fed. It is reported that one of the temples around 3000 B.C. was giving bread and beer each day to twelve thousand people. While bread and beer were all right for everyday use, special feasts could have included meat, fish, dates, and other treats.

Cylinder seals tell about the life of the people. These stone seals are carved with designs that, when the cylinder is rolled on wet clay, provide pictures of scenes such as prisoners of war, cattle attacked by lions, or priestly ceremonies. The seals varied in size from 1 to 3 inches (2.5 to 7.6 centimeters) in length. In thickness, they measured from the width of a thumb to that of a pencil. The seals were pierced lengthwise so that they could be worn on a string around the neck. People, most of whom could not read or write, could use these seals as a signature to identify possessions or to agree to contracts.

Perhaps the most remarkable invention of the Sumerians is writing and counting. They are believed to have been the first people to develop these skills. As they came to have more possessions, keeping track of things became a problem. It is thought that at first the farmers may have kept different shaped, small clay tokens as an inventory of their goods—perhaps a little sphere for a certain amount of grain, an egg shape for an animal, a cylinder for a jar of oil. When archaeologists came across these tokens, they tried to guess what they might be. Were the spheres marbles? Could the discs be lids? Were the pyramids part of a game? From the simply shaped tokens, new forms were developed with markings that may have indicated a specific kind of grain or animal. Later drawing a picture of the item on a small clay tablet, using a reed to make the markings, seemed more efficient. But curves are awkward to make with these writing materials, and pictures came to be used for a number of ideas that are otherwise hard to portray. The sign for a foot might be simplified by eliminating the curves. Then it also might be used for ideas such as stand, go, and bring. Then some scribe began to use the picture signs for sounds. Now with about six hundred characters (one-third of the number needed for the earlier picture signs), people could describe anything in their spoken language.

In order not to smudge the clay on which they had already written, the Sumerians developed a system of writing in horizontal rows from left to right—the form being used now in this book. The reed point was cut to make a wedge-shaped impression on the clay. The Sumerian form of writing is called *cuneiform,* which is Latin for "wedge shaped." Versions of this language form were used by other nations and existed as late as the first century A.D.

*Left: A sculpture of a court scribe; scribes were very important people because of their skills. Above: An example of cuneiform writing*

We take for granted the idea that the word "two" can apply to two of anything—apples, oranges, cows, buildings. However, perhaps those early tokens also led to the idea that two could be an abstract idea—one not attached to particular items. Someone looking at two tokens for grain and two tokens for animals may have seen that the idea of two could apply to anything. Merchants placed these tokens in hollow clay balls with a mark on the outside of these clay envelopes to indicate how many tokens were inside. They could send this "document" along with the goods they were shipping. Later this number mark could be combined with a picture of the item to give a system of counting.

The mathematical system developed by the Sumerians was based on the number 60. Sixty was good because it could be divided by 12 other numbers. It was used in determining the allocation of food and dividing land. It may have contributed to the development of the Arabic decimal system. We can still see traces of its influence in our 60-minute hour and the 360-degree circle.

To produce scribes who could handle words and figures,

schools were established. Not everyone went to school. Probably only the sons of wealthy families had the opportunity. Memorizing lists and copying them seems to have accounted for much of the study. The school day was from sunrise to sunset. Misbehavior was punished with a beating with a stick. It is perhaps not too surprising that we have records of students staying away from school and of a father engaging in "apple polishing" for his son by providing gifts to the teacher.

However, it is in the schools that some of the great poems and myths were written. There were stories about creation and about the great flood that occurred. There were collections of proverbs and a farmer's almanac telling farmers what to do at certain seasons. The most famous piece of literature is the *Epic of Gilgamesh*. In the story, Gilgamesh was a kind of god man who meets an uncivilized hunter named Enkidu. After fighting, the two make friends and go off to see the world. Enkidu offends the gods and is struck down with a long, painful disease from which he dies. Gilgamesh goes in search of immortality. He is supposed to have found it in a plant that grew at the bottom of the ocean. On his way home, when he was asleep, a snake steals the plant, and Gilgamesh is left with the prospect of dying the same as humans.

Also, Gilgamesh was the name of one of the early kings of the city-state of Uruk. We do not know the relationship of the hero in the epic to this ruler. The kings governed the city-states, which consisted of the city proper, suburbs, nearby towns, and the gardens, palm groves, and grainfields around them. Lagash, one of the largest, included 1,800 square miles (4,662 square kilometers) and had a population of thirty thousand to thirty-five thousand people. Sumerians may have had fourteen major cities with other

*Left: An archaeologist works on a dig in Uruk.*
*Above: A painted clay jar made in about 3000 B.C.*

areas also under their influence. The two major economic units and employers were the temple and the palace. However, from contracts found on some of the clay tablets, we learn that there also was private property.

Society was composed of three groups. At the bottom were the slaves from prisoners of war and some who sold themselves or their children because of their poverty. This group was never very large. Then there were the workers who had no land, but were employed by the temple or palace. On top were a large group of landowners that included persons from sellers of clothing to the royal family.

The ruler was considered the "shepherd" who had been chosen by the gods and who was responsible to the gods for the safety and prosperity of the city-state. The wife of the ruler played an important role in public. We have the record of one who administered the temple of the chief goddess. The ruler would have had responsibility for the upkeep of the temple and for the defense of the walls that surround the city.

At first, councils of elders had an important role in government, while the ruler did not have a lifetime job. In one council of war, there were two houses or groups: the elders and the males who would do the fighting. The elders voted conservatively not to go to war. The king did not agree and went to the other group, the fighting men. They voted for war and freedom. Indeed, the idea of "freedom" was first expressed by the Sumerians.

As the kings gained greater power, they achieved lifetime positions and chose their own successors, thus founding dynasties. One important function of the king was to go through a ritual on New Year's Day to insure prosperity for the city. In a festival celebration, the king climbed to the top of the ziggurat. There a symbolic marriage was performed with a priestess representing Inanna, the goddess of fertility, who would then bless the city with good crops.

The king presided over a bureaucracy that busied itself with programs for new canals, temples, and roads. Some cities had the beginning of postal services. Taxes had to be collected. Laws were developed to deal with commercial activities and civil and criminal violations.

That the kings must have lived in luxury can be judged from objects found in the Royal Tombs of Ur. The gold helmet of the king, the gold crown of the queen, the gold and lapis lazuli statue of a ram caught in a thicket, and the gold and silver animal heads that decorated the harps attest to a rich court life.

These tombs also contain the death pit for as many as seventy-four attendants. These soldiers and court ladies were beautifully clothed and apparently drugged or poisoned from cups found

*Ruins of the Royal Tombs of Ur*

near their skeletons before they were covered by dirt. One of the court ladies was not wearing the headband found on the others. The silver band was discovered rolled up nearby. Perhaps she had been late to her own funeral and had not had time to take it out of her pocket. Nowhere else in Mesopotamia, with one possible exception, has a tomb like this one with burials of attendants been found. Also, the only written record of a king and his court being buried together is found in one epic about the death of Gilgamesh. This type of burial may not have been usual for the Sumerians.

The constant and ruthless warfare of the city-states proved to be the reason for the defeat of the Sumerian civilization. Fights over water rights and power finally left two of the city-states at war with the others taking sides. King Eannatum of Lagash claimed dominion over all of Sumer and boasted of killing thirty-six hundred of his enemies. A few generations later, Lugalzaggisi of Umma took revenge on Lagash. He conquered the city and burned its temple. In turn, he was captured and put in a neck stock. A new civilization, the Akkadians, appeared and took over the territory of Sumer and extended its boundaries.

## AKKADIAN CIVILIZATION

Sargon the Great, who conquered Lugalzaggisi, was the king of the Akkadians. The Akkadians spoke a different language than the Sumerians—as different as Latin and Chinese. They did adapt the cuneiform system of writing to their language. The Sumerians do not appear to have borrowed many words from the Akkadians. Had the Akkadians always lived with the Sumerians? There are no Sumerian texts that describe the Akkadians as enemies, invaders, or nomads. By comparing the names derived from the two languages, we can guess that the Akkadians were stronger in the northern part of the country but a minority in the south.

Although the Akkadian rule was brief (about two hundred years), it unified the country and pushed the boundaries out to the Mediterranean Sea and down to the gulf. No longer would the city-states be considered the political unit that exercised control. Sargon, whose reign was fifty-five years (about 2334-2279 B.C.), gave the Mesopotamians the taste for empire.

Sargon came from humble origins to become cup bearer, an important post, to a Sumerian king of the city-state of Kish. The stories and myths that later were told about this hero had him being born in secret and placed in a reed basket sealed with bitumen, floated down the river, and discovered by a man drawing water who raised him as his son. Sargon's Sumerian king may have been conquered by Lugalzaggisi. In any event, Sargon's first target was this conqueror.

Then Sargon moved to the south where he washed his weapons

*A human-headed, winged bull, stands 16 feet (4.8 meters) high and weighs 40 tons (36.2 metric tons). It stood outside the throne room of the Assyrian king Sargon II.*

symbolically in the gulf. He completed his conquest of southern Sumer and then headed west and north to the Mediterranean. Next he fought to the east of Sumer. The statues and inscribed stone pillars, called *stelai* (*stele*, singular), which record these actions, stop before the end of his reign.

Controlling such a territory was tougher than conquering it. Sargon appointed Akkadians to top administrative posts and stationed Akkadian troops in the cities. He kept a large court at which he claimed fifty-four hundred persons ate daily. Not far from the city of Kish where he began his career, he built his capital called Agade to which gifts and tribute came from the far corners of his empire. Although he put Akkadians in charge, he respected the religious traditions of the Sumerians. His daughter became the priestess of Nanna, the moon god of Ur, and he became the anointed priest of other gods of the Sumerians.

Sargon's son, Rimush, repressed revolts that broke out, but he reigned only nine years. He was replaced by Manishtusu, perhaps his twin brother. Manishtusu is reported to have led an expedition across the gulf and conquered thirty-two kings of cities there (Persia or Oman) and seized the territory as far as the silver mines. Indeed the need for a source of metal may have been the reason for the expedition.

The son of Manishtusu, Naram-Sin, looked to the metal sources of the north and fought to reopen these trade routes. This grandson of Sargon was a hero who was honored as a god. A famous stele now in a museum shows him climbing up over the corpses of his enemies. He was the last great Akkadian king.

The pattern of the rise and fall of the Akkadian Empire was typical of many of the empires that followed. The rapid expansion of the conqueror was followed by rebellions, palace infighting, and frontier wars. A country with a civilization based on agriculture and metalworking required peace at home and on the trade routes. As the riches from the empire flowed into the capital, they aroused bickering among the leaders and envy of the poorer shepherds and hunters from the hill country. The empire then became vulnerable to attack by outsiders.

The Akkadian Empire changed the history of the territory. No longer would the city-states be more important than the centralized power of larger areas. The Akkadian language, art, and legends spread throughout the empire. There was greater realism in art, which now provided portraits rather than the more conventional figures. Private property and the large royal holdings undercut the power of the Sumerian temples. The Akkadian and Sumerian populations became mixed, and the later civilizations did not represent a return to the earlier Sumerian one.

*A part of the stele of Ur-Nammu*

## NEO-SUMERIAN PERIOD

The Akkadians were upset by the Guti, a people who then ruled for about one hundred years. Not much is known about this period. However, the Sumerian city of Ur was to flourish again under the leadership of Ur-Nammu. He restored some law and order. It is from his reign that we have what is considered the oldest collection of laws. He built many structures in the city including a great ziggurat. Another builder of this era was Gudea, who erected fifteen temples in the city of Girsu.

Ur-Nammu was succeeded by his son Shulgi and his grandson Amar-Sin. These two ruled over an empire that extended at least as far as the Akkadian Empire, but was better controlled. Won by battle and diplomacy, the territory was divided into administrative units over which officials were appointed by the king and transferred as the king wished. Royal inspectors were sent out to report on the government, and military power was placed in the hands of other persons appointed by the king. Communication with the far points of the empire was carried over roads guarded by fortresses along which royal messengers and traders could pass with greater safety. State ownership and operation of enterprises assumed greater importance than under the Akkadians. Serfs who worked for the state increased in numbers. The bureaucrats and the temples gained power. There were no civil wars to threaten internal fighting.

The threat came from the frontier where the Amorites, who were considered barbarians by the Sumerians, were beginning to attack. Right after the coronation of a new king of Ur on the death of his father, the empire just disintegrated, with sections declaring their independence. The cause of this rapid decline is not known. However, another group, the Elamites decided to take advantage of the situation and joined the Amorites in their attacks. About 2000 B.C., the Elamites attacked Ur, breached the walls, sacked the city, and burned it down. The king was taken prisoner.

The nomads continued to pour into the territory and established power bases where they settled. In doing so, they completely upset the state and temple control of the land. The new kings gave away, or rented for indefinite periods, the lands they now controlled. They did away with taxes and forced labor. They encouraged private property and enterprise. Big farmers, free citizens, and the merchants had new economic power. Sumer, with its city-states and its gods who owned the land and gave orders, was dead. Sumerian culture lived on in the language of the literature that was honored by the barbarians. For about two centuries (around 2000-1800 B.C.), the territory was split into four factions. In the south, the kingdoms of Isin and Larsa vied for Ur and control over Sumer and Akkad. And in the north, Assur and Eshnunna fought for control of the northern trade routes. It was Hammurabi, king of Babylon, who was to conquer the four kingdoms, unify Mesopotamia, and found the next great empire.

# Chapter 3

# WONDERS OF THE
#              ANCIENT WORLD

---

Iraq continued to be at the center of civilizations. It is difficult to comprehend for how long a period of time this land was a key player in the clash of empires. We have already covered seventeen hundred years from the time the Sumerians gathered in the city-states to 1800 B.C. when the Babylonian Empire was formed. But some of the greatest triumphs were still ahead.

## BABYLONIAN EMPIRE

Hammurabi inherited from his father a comparatively small kingdom, only 80 miles (129 kilometers) long and 20 miles (32 kilometers) wide, which was surrounded by more powerful states. However, in the forty-three years of his reign (1792-1750 B.C.), he conquered the other Mesopotamian kingdoms; established his capital, Babylon, in the central part of the land; and assumed the title, king of the four quarters of the world. Although we do not know the extent of his empire throughout the Near East, we do have a better idea of life in Babylon at the time

*A sculpture of Hammurabi, whose dynasty made the name Babylon, his capital, illustrious.*

*This sculpture was made from a cast, the original of which is in La Musèe National du Louvre in Paris.*

of Hammurabi than we have of life in some European countries of only one thousand years ago. Libraries of clay tablets that have been unearthed and monuments that have been discovered reveal Hammurabi as a skilled diplomat with a concern for justice and the welfare of the people he governed.

Most famous is the Code of Hammurabi. Although it is no longer considered the oldest code of laws in existence, it is the most complete for that age. The code is not as its name suggests, a collection of statutes adopted by some legislature. Rather it is a collection of the decisions of the king, which Hammurabi ordered carved on stone toward the end of his reign and placed in temples to show that he had administered justice. It dealt with at least 282 different decisions. Punishment was harsher than it had been with the Sumerians. Now death, mutilation (such as putting out an eye), and corporal punishment replaced compensation in kind or with money. Moreover, the punishments differed depending on whether the victim was a free person, a state worker, or a slave. Still, the announced purpose of the code was to promote justice and prevent the strong from oppressing the weak.

The government established by Hammurabi involved tight control over provincial governors. But each city had an assembly of elders that dealt with local matters and the collection of taxes. The Babylonian god, Marduk, previously a minor deity, was promoted to chief god, supposedly with the cooperation of the older Sumerian gods who were said to have called Hammurabi to be king. In return, Hammurabi repaired the temples and treated the old traditions and myths with respect, reworking them to solidify his royal power.

While originally the language of the temple was Sumerian, now the Akkadian language was used in religious worship. According to one ritual, a certain prayer was to be whispered through a reed tube in Sumerian into the right ear of a bull and in Akkadian into the left ear. While religion was very important to the state and in the lives of the Babylonians, the temples did not exercise the control over the economic and social life that they had in Sumerian times.

The center of power was now the king. The palace, which had been fairly modest before, became a complex of living quarters, office space, state reception rooms, and storage areas surrounded by walls for defense. The palace at Mari, one of the outlying towns from Babylon, measured 650 by 450 feet (198 by 137 meters) and covered about 7 acres (2.8 hectares). Its architecture, construction, and decorations were famed even in ancient times. A king on the Syrian coast sent his son on a 350-mile (563-kilometer) visit to see it. It has been called by archaeologists today "the jewel of archaic Oriental architecture."

The towns and the life-style of ordinary citizens were not too different from that found in older sections of Iraq today. Shops clustered together as they do today in a modern *souk*, or shopping center. The mud-and-brick houses were plastered and whitewashed and had an inside courtyard. The family lived in the upper story while visitors and servants used the ground floor. It is a design well suited to the climate. However, Babylonian homes had an area not found today. In a narrow courtyard behind the home under a roofed area was an altar with the personal gods who protected the family. In a part of the courtyard open to the sky was a brick pavement under which was a vaulted tomb in which members of the family were buried.

Hammurabi boasted toward the end of his reign that he had made an end of war and promoted the welfare of his people and had not let anyone terrorize the population. He claimed to be the good shepherd called by the gods to look after the people of Sumer and Akkad. However, this peace and prosperity may have been based too much on the personality of one man. The centralization of power may have come too fast.

The empire began to disintegrate when Hammurabi died in 1750 B.C. His son had to put down revolts in the provinces that had been conquered and fight against foreign invasion. Five of Hammurabi's successors managed to hang on to the kingdom around Babylon without the northern and southern provinces. After about a century the kingdom fell to a new group of people, the Hittites. The Hittite conqueror did not establish a permanent settlement at Babylon. Instead another group of people, the Kassites, took over control.

We know very little about the era of the Kassites, a period of some four hundred years. It was at this time that the Kassite rulers signed treaties dividing up the country into two parts—Assyria on the north and Babylonia on the south. The works of art and the literature of this period are considered mediocre. Great effort was made to copy the old texts and group them into collections. While Babylon lost political importance, it gained cultural status. Its literature was copied into the languages of countries throughout the Near East. From the territory that is Turkey to that of Egypt, the Babylonian language was used in the courts and among the diplomats.

In the North the Assyrians managed to shake free from foreign domination. From their base in the north in control of steppe land and the trade routes to the Mediterranean countries, they also had designs on ruling in Babylonia to the south. Another group of people, the Elamites beat them to it and toppled the Kassite Dynasty there around 1200 B.C. When the Elamites withdrew their fighters, some of the local princes started a dynasty. Nebuchadrezzar I (sometimes referred to as Nebuchadnezzar) attacked and conquered Elam, bringing back to Babylon the captured statue of the god Marduk that the Elamites had taken. However, Elam was not really conquered, and Nebuchadrezzar's successors had to worry about defense against their northern neighbor, Assyria.

Assyria was surrounded by enemies, but one of the great kings, Tiglathpileser I, managed to take them on. He pushed them back and conquered Syria and reached the Mediterranean Sea. In addition, he enjoyed hunting and claimed to have killed 4 wild bulls, 10 bull elephants, 120 lions when on foot and 800 lions from his chariot, and a narwhal, called a sea horse, in the Mediterranean. However, with the murder of this monarch, the territory entered several centuries of troubles and increasing occupation by the Aramaeans. The Aramaeans also occupied and interfered with the all-important New Year festivals.

## ASSYRIAN EMPIRE

At the end of the tenth century, Assyria did not look like the great empire it was to become. Only the chaos among her enemies had preserved the country. She had lost a great deal of territory she once governed, including the income producing trade routes. The Aramaeans had their tents almost at the gates of her capital, Assur. Her boundaries marked off a narrow strip of land about 150 miles (241 kilometers) long and 50 miles (80 kilometers) wide along the Tigris River. How then could she expand to become a great empire? She was in control of her main cities. Her fighting force was the best in the world and had combat experience because of the almost constant fighting over the years of her existence. She had chariots, horses, and weapons. Moreover, unlike her neighbors, she had a ruling dynasty that had been in power for some two centuries.

The ruler who fought to liberate his country from her enemies was Abad-nirari II. He and his son conquered all of northern Iraq in the tenth century B.C. His grandson, Ashurnasirpal II, had this larger base from which to extend the empire. The Assyrians had several motives for waging wars. They wanted to defend themselves. They wanted the loot and tribute they gained from countries they conquered. They wanted to have their god, Assur, recognized as the most powerful. While a policy of terror was common for all the conquerors of early times, the Assyrians exceeded others in their boasts of torture.

Ashurnasirpal II began a great building effort, not only in Assur

*At Nimrud archaeologists discovered these carved stone sentinels that stand about twelve feet (three-and-a-half meters) high. They have the head of a man, the body of a lion, and wings of a bird.*

and Nineveh but also with a strategically placed palace at what is now Nimrud. He brought back plants and animals to his country from his expeditions. He had a canal dug to water the plain around his new palace. The huge palace at Nimrud has been excavated by archaeologists. It covered more than 6 acres (2.4 hectares) and provided rooms for ceremonial, administrative, and living quarters. There was even a kind of air-conditioning system in the living sections, since air vents were cut into the walls to permit some circulation of air. The palace was guarded by statues of huge bull men with wings. While the wooden decorations were burned in the fires that destroyed the city in 612 B.C., a number of ivory and gold objects attest to the beauty of the furnishings. A great banquet was held when the palace was first opened in 879 B.C. with 69,574 guests being fed for ten days.

The son of Ashurnasirpal II, Shalmaneser III, carried on the family tradition of war by fighting in thirty-one of his thirty-five years of rule. A six-foot (two-meter) obelisk of black alabaster, which at the top looks like a miniature ziggurat, depicts some of the king's victories. It shows the tribute paid by heads of countries, such as King Jehu of Israel. Jehu is the first biblical person to be found in the cuneiform inscriptions by name. With stronger enemies than his father faced, Shalmaneser III did not always come away with victories. Although he conquered Babylon in an effort to block the Aramaeans from putting their candidate on the throne there, he claimed only nominal rule and left the king who had sought his help on the throne. Perhaps he was too busy with the northern and western fronts of his empire. Toward the end of his reign, one of his sons revolted and plunged the country into a civil war for four years until another son put down the rebellion.

One of the puzzles of history is the legend of Semiramis, who was supposed to be the most beautiful, cruel, powerful, and sexy of the ancient queens. For five years, Assyria was ruled by Sammuramat, presumably the source of this legend. She was the mother of King Abad-nirari III, whose father died when he was very young. Almost nothing has been found in the Assyrian records about her. Yet a Greek historian of ancient times, Herodotus, may have received the information from Babylonian priests. He passed along the story to other Greek authors who added to it, until Semiramis was credited with building Babylon and conquering Egypt and India.

Tiglathpileser III was a powerful Assyrian ruler. He said that he crushed his enemies, smashing them like pots. He strengthened the royal power by cutting back on the authority of his lords. Provinces were treated like Assyrian districts or left with their own rulers subject to a royal supervisor. A permanent army and a good system of communication with the provinces were

*A seventh-century* B.C.
*bas-relief shows
Assyrians leading
prisoners of war
into exile.*

established. Mass exiles of population were ordered to prevent
revolts and undercut national loyalties. In Iran 65,000 people were
moved, and in southern Mesopotamia it is estimated that 154,000
were affected. Assyria was one of the most feared and hated
countries in the Near East. When Ahaz, king of Judah, called for
help from the Assyrians against forces from Israel and Damascus
(in present-day Syria), Tiglathpileser came to his rescue and took
over half of Israel. He is mentioned in the Bible for this deed.

Sargon II is another of the great Assyrian kings. The empire was
strengthened under his reign. He built on a new site near Nineveh,
now near the modern village of Khorsabad, a huge palace-temple
complex. The ziggurat was seven stories—each painted with a
different color—and circled with a spiral ramp. Yet the city was
scarcely occupied before it was abandoned when Sargon II was

*Above: Ruins of the walls of Nineveh Center: These two Assyrian officials were carved on a wall just outside the throne room of King Sargon's palace. Right: On the six sides of this clay prism, King Sennacherib recorded events from eight of his military campaigns.*

killed in war and his successor moved elsewhere. By the end of Sargon's reign, Assyria controlled the entire Fertile Crescent and parts of Iran and Asia Minor. It had access to both the Mediterranean and the gulf. It had power over the entire course of the Tigris and Euphrates rivers and the important trade routes across the land.

While his successors continued for another century, their wars were largely to defend the power and territory Assyria already had. Sennacherib is known for his attack on Judah during which he captured Lachish and laid siege to Jerusalem. Hazekiah, strengthened by the prophet Isaiah, did not capitulate. The Assyrians withdrew, although valuable tribute was exacted from Judah. On his way to attack Egypt, Sennacherib's army was hit by a plague that killed thousands of the troops. In 689 B.C., Sennacherib put down a revolt in Babylon, and unlike those before him who had treated this second city of the empire with respect, he destroyed it. In Assyria, he turned Nineveh into an important capital city. His water system of canals and aqueducts was an engineering marvel.

Sennacherib was killed in 681 B.C. by several of his own sons while he was in a temple praying. After a brief battle for the throne, Esarhaddon took over Nineveh and the empire. Sennacherib is famous for rebuilding Babylon and his attacks on Egypt, where he took possession of the royal palace at Memphis. In two years, the Egyptians rebelled, and Esarhaddon was on his way back to Egypt when he died, in 669 B.C. He had arranged three years before that his son, Ashurbanipal, should succeed him in Assyria and that another son in Babylon should have power there without the empire being divided. Ashurbanipal took over the challenge of Egypt, and this time chased the pharaoh down to Thebes, the capital of Upper Egypt. Since he was 1,300 miles (2,092 kilometers) from Assyria and in a country with a strange religion, language, and customs, he withdrew, leaving local governors in charge. When another uprising in Egypt occurred, the Assyrians for the second time conquered and looted Thebes. However, Egypt was able to take control of its country again. The brother who was assigned to govern Babylon and had cooperated for seventeen years decided to assert the claims of Babylonia to world leadership with the help of an impressive list of allies. Ashurbanipal conquered Babylon. It appeared that Ashurbanipal had conquered all the enemies he could expect to govern.

The Assyrian civilization had many achievements beyond perfecting the art of war and administration. Their sculpture, especially as found in their reliefs, was designed not so much to impress the gods, but to provide humans with a lesson of political propaganda about the importance of their kings. Intellectual achievements through the collection and translation of tablets and the attempt to classify natural phenomena in lists are impressive. A map has been found on which the country farthest to the north is called the "land where the sun is not seen," raising the question about how the Assyrians might have known about Arctic winters. Knowledge of mathematics (especially algebra), astronomy (perfecting calendars, star lists, and eclipse predictions), and medicine (diagnosis, treatments, and even prevention of illness) are remarkable.

Yet in spite of these achievements, the Assyrian Empire was to collapse suddenly in 612 B.C.—just thirty years after Ashurbanipal celebrated his triumph as the most powerful leader. Records for the last twelve years of Ashurbanipal's reign are not good. At his death, there was fighting between his two sons for the throne. The Medes with the Chaldeans, who had taken over Babylon, attacked the Assyrians and destroyed the major cities. In three years of fighting, they managed to conquer this empire that had dominated this part of the world for three centuries.

## CHALDEAN OR NEO-BABYLONIAN CIVILIZATION

The Medes took their loot from the fighting and left the Chaldeans in control of Assyria. However, the Chaldeans made no effort to rebuild the cities in the north. They put all their effort into a religious and cultural revival in the south. Babylon was now the capital of their empire. They were concerned about the Egyptian influence in the area of Syria and Palestine that blocked their trade opportunities with the West. Their king, Nebuchadrezzar II, defeated the Egyptians. The Bible tells the story of how the king of Judah ignored the warnings of the prophet Jeremiah and refused to pay tribute to the Babylonians. On March 16, 597 B.C., Jerusalem was captured, and some three thousand Jews were deported to Babylon.

*Left: A panoramic view of a model of Babylon with the temple to Marduk, the chief Babylonian god, on the left. It was called* Esagila, *"the temple that lifts the head."*
*Right: Excavation at the southern palace of Nebuchadrezzar in Babylon*

The independence of this empire was brief. However, from 612 B.C. when the Assyrians were toppled, to 589 B.C. when Cyrus, king of the Persian Empire, captured Babylon, this empire created a remarkable capital city. A revival of the ancient religion sparked a rebuilding campaign. Temples again emerged as a major social and economic force. Babylon contained 500 acres (202 hectares), over 1,000 temples, and a population estimated to be about 100,000. The top of the walls surrounding the city could provide a path for two chariots each, with four horses abreast. The walls did not keep out the Persians who, with the probable help of persons inside the city, entered thrugh the bed of the Euphrates River at low water and surprised the defenders.

Eight impressive gates led into the city. The Ishtar Gate was covered with blue enameled bricks decorated in relief with red-and-white dragons and bulls symbolizing gods. A large basalt statue of a lion trampling on a man has come to be known as "the lion of Babylon," although its style is foreign to the sculpture

45

A painting reconstructs the city of Babylon with the Ishtar Gate in the foreground and the Hanging Gardens of Babylon in the right background. The gate featured bulls, lions, and dragons made of enameled tiles. Inset: A close-up of the tiles depicting a lion.

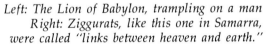

*Left: The Lion of Babylon, trampling on a man*
*Right: Ziggurats, like this one in Samarra,*
*were called "links between heaven and earth."*

characteristic of Mesopotamian civilizations.

The large throne room in the palace seems to have been decorated with animals and flowers to give the effect of beauty, rather than the massive bull men of the Assyrians designed to create awe and fear. In one part of the palace area three well shafts, probably used with a chain pump, have been discovered. Could these have watered the famous Hanging Gardens of Babylon, one of the Seven Wonders of the Ancient World? Classical authors tell us that these gardens were built by Nebuchadrezzar for his wife, the Median princess Amytis, who was homesick for the green plants of her homeland.

The great ziggurat, destroyed and rebuilt many times, was perhaps the inspiration of the Tower of Babel story from the Bible. It was a focus of the important New Year festivals carrying on the traditions of the Sumerians.

*Left: Cyrus of Persia captured Babylon in 539* B.C.
*Right: Alexander the Great's entrance into Babylon*

All this building put a heavy load of taxes on the people. A system of standardized money based on a silver standard helped to make it possible to borrow funds. Private business flourished, creating great power for some families of capitalists. The temples became important economic units and were able to keep alive the civilization even after Babylon fell to the Persians. The Persians tried to return the city to normal functioning after the war, and Cyrus worshiped the Babylonian god, Marduk. Cyrus proclaimed himself a successor to the Chaldean rulers. Babylon continued to be a great city, if not the capital of an empire. It was not until the seventh century A.D. that it was abandoned and buried beneath sand and river mud.

## DECLINE AND DEATH OF THE ANCIENT MESOPOTAMIAN CIVILIZATION

Throughout this long period of history down to the 539 B.C. capture of Babylon by Cyrus of Persia, there had been a continuity in ideas and customs that developed in the "Land Between Two Rivers." Now with foreign domination that did not make this territory central to their empires and purposes, the civilization lost out to others and eventually became forgotten.

The Achaemenian, or Persian Period, began in 539 B.C. with the new kings still looking after some of the royal duties of this territory. However, the successors to Cyrus were more concerned with fighting the Egyptians and then the Greeks. Efforts of the Babylonians to regain their independence were crushed. Buildings in the south were not rebuilt and the north was still in ruins from the Assyrian defeat. The cost of living rose sharply, creating economic problems. With the mixture of populations introduced, the Persians made Aramaic the language of their empire. Soon only the scholars and scribes could read the Akkadian and Sumerian languages in the cuneiform script. The common people lost their native language and the key to their history. The Babylonians adopted names of foreign gods whom they now turned to worship.

Alexander the Great brought the Greek Empire to the territory, beginning the Hellenistic Period. The Persian armies surrendered Babylon without a fight. Alexander was greeted as a liberator and accepted as a king. He offered sacrifices to Marduk and ordered the rebuilding of the temples, although this task was not completed. He stayed in Babylon for a month before resuming his campaign that would take him into India. When he returned, he had great plans for making the city one of the capitals of his empire and a great port after the Euphrates River had been made navigable to the gulf. However, Alexander's death in Babylon at the age of thirty-two in 323 B.C., probably from malaria, cut short these dreams.

Alexander's successors were not able to hold together his empire. The Greeks founded their own cities in the area, and the

*A new temple has been built on the remains of an ancient temple in Babylon.*

center of culture and political importance shifted to the Mediterranean. However, the temples continued to preserve the ancient learning, and the Greeks learned some of the Babylonian science and astrology.

Then the territory was claimed by the Parthians in the end of the second century B.C. and the Sassanians from Persia who fought the Roman and Byzantine empires from the west in the third century A.D. The Sassanians developed a centralized control of the river systems for irrigation and travel. They built the city of Ctesiphon on the trade routes between East and West. The remains of the palace with the arch of the huge vaulted hall still impresses travelers today. The Romans captured the city twice, but were not able to hold it. The Sassanians attempted to replace the worship of the gods in this territory with their own faith. They attacked the Jews and Christians who were not living in this territory. However it was the new religion of Islam that was to overwhelm this empire and start a new era for this ancient country.

# Chapter 4

# ISLAM'S INFLUENCE

Islam, the religion preached by Muhammad, was to be a major factor in the civilizations that arose after the Arabs introduced it into the territory that is now Iraq. Muslim civilization at Baghdad under the Abbasids represented the center for philosophical, scientific, and literary achievements unmatched elsewhere at that time.

## ARAB CONQUEST

The Arabs, energized by the teaching of the prophet Muhammad, conquered the Persians in A.D. 637. Muhammad lived in the territory that is now Saudi Arabia. The revelations he received are collected in the Muslim holy book, the Koran. When Muhammad died in 632, there was a crisis over who should be his successor. Several of the competing factions accepted sixty-year-old Abu Bakr, the prophet's earliest follower outside of his family. He was given the title of *caliph*, which means successor. Some, however, felt that the title should have gone to the nearest male relative, Muhammad's son-in-law Ali, who had married Muhammad's daughter Fatimah and fathered the only grandsons of the prophet.

*Ptolemy, an astronomer and geographer, drew this map of the known world around 100 A.D. The triangular section of land near the center (with the word ARABIA near the top), is the Arabian Peninsula. Above it are Babylonia, Mesopotamia, and Assyria.*

Abu Bakr sent out the troops to deal with those among the Arab tribes who felt they were released from loyalty by the death of Muhammad. When Abu Bakr died and Umar ibn al-Khattab, another of Muhammad's close companions, became caliph, the mission of Islam became a *jihad*, a holy war against unbelievers. The tough Arab fighters were small in numbers but they outmaneuvered the Byzantine and Persian empires, taking both Jerusalem and Ctesiphon in the year 637. They pressed on across Persia and in a few more years had advanced into India. Umar, ruling from Medina in the Arabian Peninsula, let the people he had conquered keep their own laws and religious beliefs. Often the people found the taxation lighter and the justice better.

Umar was stabbed to death by a Persian slave with a poisoned dagger. Umar had made arrangements for the selection of his successor, who was Uthman. The dynasty founded by Uthman is called Umayyad (sometimes Ommiad).

Uthman continued to expand the territory of his rule, but the decade of the major gains of land was over. Umar had lived a simple life sleeping on a bed of palm leaves and wearing the same wool robe for years. Uthman had to rule over a new empire and appointed relatives of his Umayyad clan to positions of power. The appointments were resented. The first revolt came in 655 at Kufa near Ctesiphon. Then Uthman's opponents demanded the resignation of Uthman. When he refused, they took his palace and killed him.

The next caliph chosen was Ali, who had lost the first election. This choice was opposed by Aishah, the prophet's widow, who was joined by two of the leaders from Mecca (in present-day Saudi Arabia). The three went to Basra (in present-day southern Iraq) where they raised an army. Ali went to Kufa and picked up more supporters to add to his own force and then went to Basra where, in the Battle of the Camel, he defeated his opposition. It was the first major clash between Muslims.

Uthman's cousin, Muawiyah, who ruled in Damascus, thought that Ali had not tried to bring the killers of his relative to justice. He brought an army against Ali in the town of Siffin on the Euphrates. When Ali was winning at first, Muawiyah had his warriors stick pages from the Koran on their spears and go forward with the cry, "Let God decide." Since a Muslim could not strike down the Koran, Ali was bested in the fight, forced to submit the matter to arbitration, and had to retreat to Kufa. Ali's prestige was hurt. A group of former supporters revolted and killed Ali in 661.

Islam was now the largest empire. Muawiyah put himself forward as a candidate to be the next caliph. Ali's eldest son was persuaded to give up his claim by the offer of a lifelong income in Medina, where he is reported to have married and divorced some ninety women before he died at forty-five years of age. Muawiyah was accepted as caliph and became the first in the Umayyad line that ruled for a century from Damascus. The eldest son was named to succeed with the approval of the advisers and tribal leaders, as was the custom of the desert tribes.

Numbers of non-Muslims converted to avoid the heavier taxes imposed on those who were not of the Islamic faith. Thus the rulers were forced to tax all subjects alike. Arabic became the official language. Many books that were discovered in other languages were translated into Arabic. In this way some of the Greek classics that would have been lost because of the chaotic political situation in the West were preserved. The boundaries of the Umayyads stretched from China across North Africa and up through Spain to within 100 miles (161 kilometers) of Paris, France.

Controversy still existed about the rightful claims to the caliphate. Ali's second son, Husain, and the only living grandson of the prophet Muhammad, was trying to join some rebels in the territory of Iraq. In 680 near the city of Karbala they were opposed by a government force that wiped them out. Husain's head was cut off and sent to Damascus. This act led to the formation of a political party that opposed the Umayyads. The party, known as the Shiat Ali or Party of Ali, was to become the Shiites, one of the two largest divisions in Islam. The other group, the Sunnis, are the largest unit of the mainstream orthodox Muslims. Many of the Shiite shrines are located in Iraq at the scene of events that are important in the lives of Ali and Husain.

Another challenge of the caliphate came at a time of increasing unhappiness with the corruption and worldliness of the Umayyads. The family descended from Abbas, uncle of Muhammad, and therefore a proper candidate from the Shiite view that the caliph should be from the prophet's family, claimed

power and leadership of the Sunnis. In 750 the Abbasids, as the
family was known, overthrew the Umayyads. They transferred
the capital of their empire from Damascus to Baghdad.

## THE ABBASIDS

Abu al-Abbas founded a line of rulers that was to last until
1258. His caliphate was to be a return to the religiously oriented
state from the more secular one of his predecessors.

The successor to Abbas, al-Mansur, was to found the capital of
Baghdad. Within a century that city was estimated to have a
population of a million. The city was built on a circular plan with
three walls and a double moat. The caliph's palace had a golden
dome and a golden gate. The palace boasted a solid silver tree with
branches of silver and gold and leaves of various colors. On these
were mechanical birds of various types that sang or cooed, while
the branches moved as if a breeze were blowing.

It is no wonder that centuries of people have been fascinated by
the stories of life at this time recorded in *The Book of The Thousand
and One Nights* (sometimes called the *Arabian Nights*). According
to that classic, a beautiful girl, Sheherazade, was able to save her

*The Ali Baba Fountain in Baghdad shows Ali Baba's female slave, Murjana. She killed the thieves who were after Ali Baba by pouring boiling oil into the jars in which the thieves were hiding.*

life by telling her husband such wonderful stories that he could not kill her until he heard the ending the following night, at which time she started a new story. It is from this book that we have the tales of Aladdin and the Magic Lamp, Ali Baba and the Forty Thieves, and The Voyages of Sindbad the Sailor, and others.

Baghdad was also the intellectual capital of the world. It reached its height under the well-known Caliph Harun al-Rashid in the eighth century at a time when Europe was still in the Dark Ages. Translations from Greek, Persian, and Indian sources enriched the minds of scholars. Theology and law were important studies. Significant gains were made in medicine and pharmacology. Hospitals were established at Baghdad and in the provinces. The scholars excelled in astronomy and mathematics. Music was appreciated. Although according to some people the Islamic tradition does not allow artists to make images of animate objects, Islamic art found expression in intricate designs.

New forms of religious expression were developed that were strikingly different. The Order of Assassins was led by one who taught that if his followers were killed in assassinating enemies, they would be guaranteed a life in paradise. The Sufis, on the other hand, developed a teaching stressing love, inner guidance, and ascetic practices as a way of knowing God and ultimately gaining union with God. Several important Sufi orders, or groups, are based in Iraq and trace their origin to the Abbasid period.

Baghdad became the center for Middle Eastern trade. Merchants placed their products on ships that sailed to India, Sri Lanka (then Ceylon), and China. Camel caravans took land routes to Baghdad from Persia, Arabia, Egypt, Syria, and beyond. However, the old pattern of inner divisions and rebellions in the provinces repeated itself. Religious persecutions against Muslim groups considered unorthodox and against the Jews and the Christians were instituted. An uprising of black slaves in the swamps of the delta region of the rivers engaged military resources at the very time that outlying regions were rebelling.

The Buyids, a Shiite family of Persian origin, seized power while leaving the Sunni caliph in place. One of the rulers, Adud al-Dawlah tried to improve the roads, canals, and postal system. He encouraged trade. The Buyids adopted a system of paying troops with land free of taxes. That practice undermined the financial strength of the empire. Also, these rulers were unable to prevent outsiders from attacking even Baghdad and terrorizing the residents.

It was then that a Sunni family of Turkish origin, the Seljuqs, took over. Toghril Beg conquered Baghdad in 1055 and ousted the Buyids by 1059. The Sunni caliph gave over all political power to the Seljuqs. In an effort to restore orthodoxy, the Sunni family founded colleges for the training of officials in religious and secular matters. One of the most famous, Nizamiya, was founded in 1067 at Baghdad, although the family chose to rule from other

*Tamerlane conquered Baghdad twice—in 1393 and again in 1401.*

cities as their capitals. In the south, there were Shiite families with strong local power. Religious disputes and power plays further weakened central control. Although the Crusades from the nations of the West had been repelled successfully, a threat came from another direction—the Mongols.

## THE MONGOLS

The grandson of Genghis Khan, Hulagu, who had power over Persia, invited the Abbasid caliph to surrender. When the caliph refused, Hulagu conquered Baghdad in 1258 after a siege of seven weeks. The city was sacked, and large numbers of people were put to death. Artistic and cultural treasures were destroyed or taken away. The canal system on which agriculture depended was allowed to fail. The country was devastated and was unable to regain its strength until the twentieth century.

Another band of Mongols under Tamerlane (also called Timur)

*Sulayman the Magnificent*

conquered Baghdad in 1393 and again in 1401. The city went
through another siege of destruction and killing of the
inhabitants. Throughout this period of chaos, Bedouin tribes in
the south and the tribes of the Turkomans and Kurds in the north
revolted against outside power. Religious tensions among the
groups continued with different factions attempting to seize
power. With a strong Ottoman Turkish empire building in the
West, it was not long before the Ottomans extended their control
over the area of Iraq.

## THE OTTOMANS

It was a leader of the Kurds whose revolt the Persian tried to
put down that sparked the showdown between the Persian rulers
and the great Ottoman (Turkish) leader, Sulayman the
Magnificent. Sulayman captured Baghdad in the 1530s and, except
for a brief period of Persian control, the Ottomans held the land
that was to become Iraq until 1918.

At first the Ottomans were able to give the people of this territory the first stable government in centuries. However, wars with the Persians and the weakening of the administrative system of the central government left the people at the mercy of local leaders and dynasties. Arabian tribes from the west and Kurdish tribes from Persia and the east poured into the country. The added population increased the fighting for land and water.

Then in the eighteenth century, Iraq was ruled by Mamelukes. Mamelukes were slaves from among the non-Muslims who were trained to be administrators for the Ottomans. They had been used successfully in other parts of the empire. In Iraq they produced a number of outstanding rulers, Hasan Pasha, Sulayman II, and Abd ar-Rahman al-Daud, who made important reforms in the legal system, cleared the canals, and started industry. When the Ottomans sought to replace Daud in 1831, he refused. An army was sent from Istanbul, the Ottoman capital, to capture Baghdad. Daud was beaten, but probably as much by two natural catastrophes as by the army—a plague that killed thirty thousand people and a flood that devastated much of the city.

Gaining control over the various tribal leaders was no easy task. One of the strongest of the governors, Midhat Pasha, introduced reforms in providing a voice for local people in government, establishing a system of education outside the mosques, and the settlement of the tribes with a land registration system. He started newspapers, hospitals, and banks. The Western powers of Europe began to take an interest in the area. The chief rivals were the Germans, who had a contract to build a railroad, and the British, who had interests in the oil of Persia.

When the Ottoman Turks sided with Germany in World War I, the British sent in troops that conquered Baghdad. The British

*Midhat Pasha (left) and Prince Faisal (right)*

announced their intention to return to Iraq some control over its country, which had been under foreign domination since the Mongol invasion in the thirteenth century. While some Arab nationalists, such as Jafar al-Askari, Nuri as-Said, and Jamil al-Midfai, had wanted the Ottomans overthrown, most of the local people showed little interest in the fighting.

## THE BRITISH MANDATE

At the peace conferences following World War I, the Allied powers decided to divide up and rule the former Ottoman territories. Iraq and Palestine were placed under British control, while Syria and Lebanon were given to the French. Prince Faisal was from an Arab family who traced their ancestry back to the prophet Muhammad, and he had been proclaimed king of Syria in 1920 by the Syrian Congress. The French did not agree with this plan and had Faisal deported from Syria. Since Faisal's father and

*Faisal, king of Iraq, visited England in 1933. Left: Leaving his hotel to visit King George; Right: Inspecting British navy troops at Dover, England*

family had fought for the Allies, the British invited him to come to London. Prince Faisal was to become the first king of Iraq, in 1921.

The British faced a country in great need of rebuilding. The country still suffered from the usual divisions of town against tribe, merchants against debtors, and Sunnis against Shiites. For three months, a revolt against the British had the country in turmoil. In October 1920, a temporary Arab government was established to be assisted by British advisers and answerable to the British high commissioner for Iraq, Sir Percy Cox. A referendum was held to see whether the people would support Prince Faisal to be their king. As a descendant of the prophet Muhammad and as one who had fought for Arab nationalism and supported the British in World War I, he had the background that was considered important for leadership. The British modified somewhat their powers under the Mandate Agreement of the Allies. In 1929 they agreed to terminate the mandate entirely and support the entry of Iraq in the League of Nations.

# Chapter 5

# FREE AT LAST

For centuries Iraq had been under foreign rule. The interest in the formation of national states that was strong in World War I made possible the formation of Iraq.

## THE MONARCHY

With the admission of Iraq to the League of Nations, the British Mandate terminated. Iraq became a sovereign, independent state. Moreover, with the discovery of oil at Naft Khaneh in 1923 and at Kirkuk in 1927 and with the export of oil products by 1930, the government had revenues to support its work.

While many of the traditional tensions between groups continued, the problem of the Kurds intensified. At the end of World War I, there had been a conditional agreement between the Allies and Turkey to establish an independent Kurdish state, Kurdistan, with territory taken from Iraq, Turkey, and Iran. Because of changed political conditions in Turkey, the plan was not put into effect. In 1926 when the League of Nations awarded the city of Mosul to Iraq rather than Turkey, the Kurdish areas were brought into the Iraqi state. Some Kurds have continued to demand self-determination.

*King Ghazi, who liked to drive fast cars, was killed in an auto crash in Baghdad.*

King Faisal I ruled from 1921 to 1933. He was succeeded by his son, King Ghazi, who had difficulty in providing leadership in resolving the claims of various factions at the very time that there was increasing demand for government reforms and improvements of conditions in the country. The military began to take an active role in politics, beginning in 1936 with a coup d'etat in which the army forced out the elected government and killed the minister of defense, but left the king in place. After several more coups, the politicians and military split into two major groups. One group was pro-British and was led by Nuri as-Said. The other was pro-German led by Rashid Ali al-Gailani. In 1939 King Ghazi died, leaving his crown to his four-year-old son Faisal II, whose uncle, Abd al-Ilah, became the regent and crown prince.

During World War II, the pro-British faction sided with the Allies while the pro-German faction had sympathies with the Axis powers. When Rashid Ali tried to return to power in a coup and

*In 1958 representatives from Jordan and Iraq met in Jordan to discuss the Arab Federation.*

modify a 1930 treaty with Britain concerning wartime conditions, the British landed military forces in Iraq. The Iraqi army received some support from the Axis powers. The British put down the fighting, and the later governments cooperated with the Allies. Iraq declared war on the Axis powers in 1943.

In 1945 Iraq was one of the founding members of the Arab League, which provided a loose framework for Arab unity with Egypt, Jordan, Lebanon, Saudi Arabia, Syria, and Yemen. Iraq joined the United Nations in 1945. When there was concern about the rising power of the Soviet Union, Iraq signed a mutual defense treaty with Turkey, and later Iran and Pakistan, called the Baghdad Pact. In 1958 Iraq joined with Jordan in the formation of the Arab Federation that was to counter the anti-Western United Arab Republic that had been formed earlier by Egypt and Syria.

Within Iraq, the two strong leaders were recognized as Nuri as-Said and the Crown Prince Abd al-Ilah. King Faisal II became eighteen in 1953 and came to power. Many of the leaders of reform movements felt that the governing powers were hostile to ideas for improvements. Wealth was concentrated in the hands of a few, especially large landholders in the countryside. Nuri as-Said banned all political parties in 1954. Greater opposition developed, especially after the French and British attacked Egypt in 1956. Many people resented the regime's ties to the West because of Western support for Israel. The opposition wanted to reduce foreign influence and end the Baghdad Pact.

In the revolution of 1958, the monarchy was overthrown and Nuri as-Said, Crown Prince Abd al-Ilah, and King Faisal II, together with other members of the royal family, were killed. The coup had been led by two army officers, Brigadier General Abd al-Karim Qasim and Colonel Abd as-Salam Arif. Small units, or cells, in the military plotted the coup. Baghdad was captured on July 14, 1958.

## THE REVOLUTIONARIES

Qasim, as head of the Revolutionary forces, formed a cabinet over which he presided. Iraq was declared a republic with Islam as the state religion. A constitution announced that Iraq was a part of the Arab nation, with Arabs and Kurds as partners in the homeland. Arif, with whom Qasim had plotted the overthrow of the government, was soon out of favor because he was associated with the powerful political party, the Baath party. Also, he supported the union of Iraq with the United Arab Republic. Arif was accused of plotting against the interests of Iraq.

Qasim withdrew Iraq from the Baghdad Pact. He moved to limit the influence of Communist elements in the country. The Communists had supported the Kurds through the People's

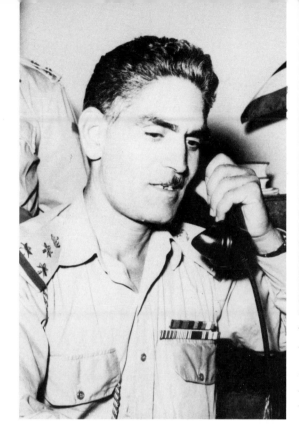

*Possessions that mobs ripped from the palace during the revolution of 1958 include a portrait of Crown Prince Abd al-Ilah and his wife (above). Abd al-Ilah was killed. After the revolution, Abd al-Karim Qasim (left) took control of the government.*

Resistance Force. When fighting broke out with the Kurds, Qasim disbanded that organization. The Kurds demanded some independent status and fought a successful guerrilla war. Qasim claimed Iraq should control Kuwait, a neighboring Arab country. This act antagonized the other Arab countries and Great Britain. Qasim clashed with the foreign-owned oil company. A law was passed to prevent the granting of oil rights to foreigners and to transfer control over all oil matters to the Iraq National Oil Company. Qasim remained friendly on the international front only with the Soviet Union. Because of his dictatorship, in 1963 the army and the Baath party cooperated to overthrow Qasim, who was executed.

Colonel Arif, who had been in disfavor, was now made president with Brigadier General Ahmad Hasan al-Bakr forming a cabinet favoring Arab unity, socialism, and freedom. The party was divided into two groups. One favored unity with the United

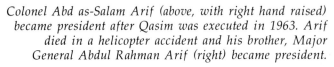

*Colonel Abd as-Salam Arif (above, with right hand raised) became president after Qasim was executed in 1963. Arif died in a helicopter accident and his brother, Major General Abdul Rahman Arif (right) became president.*

Arab Republic. The other had no enthusiasm for the Egyptian control that such a move would mean. Arif seized power with the aid of the military forces and placed some of the leaders of the Baath party under arrest. A new provisional constitution was adopted. The banks and a number of industries were nationalized. However, socialism was not that attractive to the Iraqis, and Arif was not too happy with the economic ideas that had been pushed by the pro-Egyptian element. He was moving to replace the group who wanted this approach. Arif put in Abd ar-Rahman al-Bazzaz as leader of the government, who while not doing away with socialism would work to increase production and balance private and public interests. Also, Arif was moving to return power to civilian rather than military control. Arif died in a helicopter accident in 1966.

The military placed the older brother of Arif, who was named Abdul Rahman Arif, in power. Arif reversed the plans and dismissed Bazzaz. Tensions with Western nations over support of Israel in the Arab-Israeli War of 1967 led Iraq to break off relations with the United States and Britain. Two years of factions fighting for power within the military finally resulted in the Baath party and other opposition parties calling for a coalition government and the holding of elections for the Assembly.

Arif refused the demands for elections. Once again the military stepped in with a coup, and General Ahmad Hasan al-Bakr became president. Arif went into exile. This transfer of power took place on July 17, 1968. A Revolutionary Command Council was established. Almost immediately two factions who split on issues of socialism and other matters were at odds. Under the direction of the Baath party, one group was removed on July 30, 1968 by a group of officers led by Saddam Husain, the man who was to succeed Bakr as president in 1979.

Between 1968 and 1979, the Baath party worked to establish better relationships with the Kurds and with the Communist party. The High Committee of the Progressive National Front was established in which the Baath party had eight seats; the Communist party, three; the Kurdish Democratic party, three; and the Progressive Nationalist and the Independent Democrats, one each. The party nationalized oil companies and entered into agreements with foreign powers for technical and economic assistance in support of the oil operations. Land distribution, irrigation projects, and labor laws were part of the reform package also. In the 1970s after oil price increases, Iraq underwent rapid development and modernization. In international relations, a treaty with the Shah of Iran was signed in 1975. The treaty was supposed to eliminate all conflict between the two countries. Iraq opposed the Camp David agreements of 1978 between Egypt and Israel. It hosted a Pan-Arab Summit in 1978, in which Arab nations agreed to apply sanctions against Egypt for signing a

*The opening session of the Pan-Arab Summit in Baghdad (right).*
*President Saddam Husain (left) speaking at a press conference in 1980*

peace treaty with Israel. Plans for complete political and economic union of Iraq and Syria were going forward until July 1979.

## SADDAM HUSAIN

On July 16, 1979, Saddam Husain replaced Bakr as president and chairman of the Revolutionary Command Council. Husain took a position of nonalignment with world powers while pleading for Arab solidarity. Husain saw himself as leader of such an Arab group.

Elections were held for membership in the Iraqi National Assembly and the Legislative Council for the Autonomous Region of Kurdistan. The Baath party remained in control. Nevertheless, the problem of the Kurds remains. Husain was unable to negotiate a resolution in order to prevent fighting against the Kurds.

In 1979 Iran underwent an Islamic revolution in which the Ayatollah Khomeini, its leader, urged Iraqi Shiites and others to

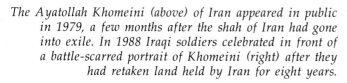

*The Ayatollah Khomeini (above) of Iran appeared in public in 1979, a few months after the shah of Iran had gone into exile. In 1988 Iraqi soldiers celebrated in front of a battle-scarred portrait of Khomeini (right) after they had retaken land held by Iran for eight years.*

overthrow the Baath government. Border fighting became frequent during 1980, and Iran ignored Iraq's efforts to settle the matter by diplomacy. War with Iran began on September 16, 1980 with Iraq's forces entering Iran.

Iranian resistance was strong and pushed Iraqi troops back to the border where the two sides were stalemated. In 1982 Husain ordered the withdrawal of his troops from Iranian soil. The Iranian troops then crossed over into Iraq and engaged in heavy fighting. Iraqi oil terminals and some pipelines were closed down with a resulting cut of 75 percent in oil revenues by 1983. When the war escalated to include attacks on shipping of oil in the gulf area, the oil supplies and the ships of other nations were in jeopardy. The United States navy then went into the gulf to help protect Kuwaiti ships that depended on the free passage of their oil tankers. At last a cease-fire was negotiated and went into effect on August 20, 1988.

Although exact figures have not been published, it is estimated that during the eight-year war, 150,000 may have died and many

*A minesweeping tugboat leads American tankers
and warships through the gulf in 1987.*

more were injured—in a male population of 8,000,000. While the
Shiite Iraqis remained loyal to their nation and suspicious of
Iran's leader, the Ayatollah Khomeini, many of the Kurds sided
with Iran thinking that country would win. With the front against
the Iranians closed, the Iraqis turned their military strength
against the Kurds, driving some 60,000 of them into Turkey for
refuge. The Iraqi use of chemical warfare in the closing days of the
war against Iran and then later against the Kurds aroused strong
international protest.

Iraq invaded neighboring Kuwait on August 2, 1990. After
failing to install a native government in Kuwait and discovering
that other Arab nations did not support the invasion, Iraq claimed
Kuwait belonged to it. Iraq then moved troops toward Saudi
Arabia. By August 6 the United Nations Security Council had
voted a trade embargo against goods entering Iraq. Saudi Arabia
invited the United States to send troops to help defend Saudi
territory and they did. The Arab League, in emergency session,
voted to condemn Iraq's action and to send troops to Saudi
Arabia.

*Egyptians who had worked in Kuwait or Iraq before the Iraqi invasion in August 1990 wait in Jordan for transportation home.*

Saddam Husain threatened to destroy Arab oil fields and attack Israel. On September 25, the United Nations Security Council voted to extend its land and sea embargo to include air traffic. The council also adopted resolutions condemning Iraq's takeover of Kuwait and told them to withdraw their troops by January 15, 1991.

Iraqi troops were not withdrawn and on January 16 a United States-led multinational allied force began air and missile attacks against Iraq. Iraq retaliated by firing scud missiles at Saudi Arabia and Israel.

On February 27 the allies began a ground attack to retake Kuwait. Iraq gave little resistance. After one hundred days the allies were declared victorious. The Gulf War was over. There was massive destruction to Iraq and its people, but Saddam Husain remained in power.

The Iraqi government submitted a required weapons inventory report to the International Atomic Energy Agency indicating that weapons-grade nuclear materials had been moved prior to the war and survived allied bombings. Omissions of nuclear material in the report indicated that inspections would be required to track down nuclear material. The embargo imposed by the United Nations remained in effect.

*The Monument to the Revolution in Baghdad is no longer standing.*

# Chapter 6

# LIFE IN IRAQ

Iraq's history is a rich one, providing everyone with some significant advances in civilization. Iraq's leaders are not willing just to glory in the past. President Saddam Husain summed up his attitude in a speech made to the Baath party's information and cultural bureau on August 11, 1977. He recognizes the past and the Islamic heritage as essential elements of society. He does not want a sharp break with this past. The reform that he wants as part of the revolution is to be a gradual change to advance the country and its role among the Arab nations.

It is easy to see the influence of both Iraq's history and development under President Husain in the structures and the culture of life today in this nation. The government, the religion, the educational systems, the arts, and the status of women all reflect the heritage of Iraq and a reaching out to the future.

## GOVERNMENT

The center of power is in the president with the Revolutionary Command Council, which in December 1987 had nine other members. The Iraq Regional Command of the Baath party also is influential in making decisions. The Council of Ministers is appointed by the president and is in charge of administrative duties of government.

Legislative authority lies mainly with the president and the Revolutionary Command Council although the National Assembly also plays some role. The Assembly has 250 members elected by all adult voters for a four-year term. No elections were held between 1958 and 1980, but three have been conducted since then in 1980, 1984, and 1989. The country has fifteen provinces (al-Anbar, al-Basrah, al-Muthanna, al-Qadisiyah, an-Najah, al-Tamim, Babil, Baghdad, Dhi Qar, Diyala, Karbala, Maysan, Ninawa, Salah ad-Din, and Wasit) and three autonomous regions (as-Sulaymaniyah, Dahuk, and Irbil). The Kurdish area has elections to a 50-member Kurdish Legislative Council. Elections for that council were held in September 1980 and August 1986.

Under the new proposed constitution, the Council of Ministries would be responsible to the National Assembly and people could form political parties. The Communist party still would be banned because of its support of Iran in the Gulf War. The possibility of abolishing the Revolutionary Command Council and having the president elected directly by the people is being discussed.

Military service is compulsory for males at age eighteen. Service is between twenty-one months and two years, but can be extended in time of war. As of July 1987, it was estimated that Iraq had an army of 955,000, an air force of 40,000, and a navy of 5,000. In addition, during the Gulf War with Iran, the regular forces were supplemented by a 650,000-member popular army and possibly as many as 10,000 volunteers from Arab countries. The army has played an influential role through coups and attempted coups in determining the leadership of the country.

The judicial system is supervised by a judicial council headed by the minister of justice. There are three separate types of courts: civil, religious, and special. The civil courts hear both civil and

*Signs in Arabic in Medics Street advertise doctors' names, their specialties, and their medical affiliations. A few signs have additional information in English.*

criminal cases. Decisions can be appealed to higher courts. The highest court is the Court of Cassation. That court also hears cases involving crimes committed by public officials. Each of the religious communities has its own religious court that considers questions of personal status, marriage, and inheritance. Special courts that have jurisdiction over cases involving state security were established in 1965. The majority of judges for cases of that type are from the military.

The Social Security Scheme introduced in 1957 was extended in 1976. Benefits are given for old age, sickness, unemployment, maternity, marriage, and death. Health services are free. Expansion of health facilities was a priority under the 1981-85 five-year plan. Thirty new hospitals were built. At the end of 1986, the country boasted 228 hospital units with a total of 32,166 beds and 6,074 physicians.

# RELIGION

While minorities are permitted to practice their religion, the state religion is Islam, and 95 percent of the Iraqis are Muslims. Islam means submission to the will of God. Islam is a monotheistic religion like Christianity and Judaism. It is based on the *shahada*: "There is no God but God (Allah), and Muhammad is his Prophet." The Koran is the holy book that contains the inspired words of Muhammad disclosed by God through the Angel Gabriel. The Muslims revere this book and believe that it contains everything humans need for salvation.

The Muslims also believe that the Christian gospels, the first five books of the Old Testament, and the psalms are inspired. However, they think that the texts available today are not as God revealed them. Muslims recognize Adam, Noah, Abraham, Moses, and Jesus as great prophets, but for them Muhammad is the last and greatest prophet.

The *Hadith* contains traditions based on sayings and deeds of Muhammad. The Koran and the Hadith provide the basis for the code of behavior that governs Muslims. That code is called the *sunna*. The two main groups of Muslims, the Sunnis and the Shiites, have different Sunna.

The basic teaching is to be found in the "Five Pillars": (1) the shahada emphasizing the oneness of God, (2) the duty to pray five times a day, (3) fasting, (4) giving to others, and (5) the pilgrimage to Mecca. The repetition of the shahada, once, aloud, with understanding and belief is necessary to become a Muslim. Prayer five times a day, facing toward Mecca in a certain way, is required. Next to the mosques, buildings set aside for group prayer and worship, are minarets, or towers, from which a person

*Opposite page: The Abu-l-Fadil al-Abbas mosque in Karbala*

*People are called to prayer from the minaret of the Ramadan Mosque in Baghdad.*

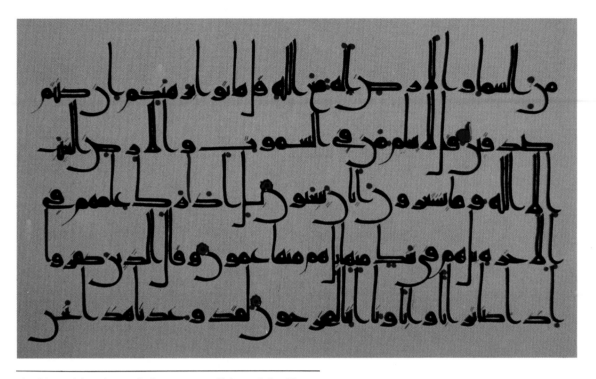

*Arabic writing in a ninth-century edition of the Koran*

(or more recently a loudspeaker) calls the people to prayer.

Friday is the day for Muslims to gather together in their mosque to pray and to hear a sermon. It is not like the Sabbath in that the Koran indicates that after listening to the sermon, Muslims should then return to their businesses. The preachers, called imams, are teachers but they are not priests with religious authority to stand between the worshiper and God.

Fasting is required during the month of Ramadan from dawn until the last light has gone from the evening sky. The fast means no food, drink, tobacco, or other worldly pleasure during the day. Since Ramadan falls at different times in the year, because it is determined by a calendar based on the moon, it takes some endurance when it falls in the heat of summer. Exceptions are made for the sick, the weak, soldiers, and travelers.

Giving to the poor and to the mosques is a religious obligation. In early Islam, it was customary to give one-fortieth of one's

*The Kaaba, the great shrine in Mecca*

amassed wealth each year. Now only a minority follow all these provisions with respect to giving.

The pilgrimage to Mecca is expected of every Muslim who can afford to go. The Kaaba is the great shrine in Mecca that is considered the center of the pilgrimage ritual. The Shiites also make a pilgrimage to one of the great Shiite holy places in Iraq.

As with other religions, observance of these obligations by the faithful varies. For a while, Muslims who had been influenced by other cultures took a more relaxed view of these requirements, and so did the poorer, working classes. However, there has been a renewed interest in orthodox observance of these requirements for the Muslims throughout the Arab world.

*The Arch of Knowledge (left) and classroom
buildings (right) at al-Mustansiriyya University*

## EDUCATION

Before 1921 there were few educational opportunities apart
from religious schools. Now education is free and compulsory for
primary school, which is six years beginning at age six. Secondary
education begins at age twelve and lasts for six years, in two series
of three years each. In 1981 it was estimated that 49 percent of the
children for this age group were in secondary schools (64 percent
boys and 36 percent girls). There are forty-six teacher training
institutes, nineteen technical institutes, and six universities.

Stamping out illiteracy was one of the goals of the government
after the revolution in 1968. In order to try to meet the needs of all
segments of the population, literacy classes were held on large
ships and oil tankers, on floating schools for the Arabs who live in
the marshes, and in traveling schools for the nomads. The country

*Young people in Iraq have ample opportunity to get a good education.*

won an award in 1979 for its literacy program from the United Nations Educational, Scientific and Cultural Organization (UNESCO).

The Iraqi efforts at education are showing results in the formation of a growing professional and middle class. Also, an educated work force has played a significant role in the country's economic development.

## THE ARTS

Iraq has a rich cultural life. The ancient traditions in architecture, sculpture, painting, weaving and carpet making, and prose and poetry have been carried on in modern achievements. The ministry of culture and information has sought to preserve the past while encouraging contemporary artists.

In Baghdad the ancient monuments exist along with modern steel, glass, and concrete buildings. Modern sculpture and painting is appreciated and statues depicting Iraqi history and

*Above: Iraqis still practice ancient crafts of shaping pottery and making copper utensils.*
*Below: A new resort for tourists (left) and a modern home (right)*

*A monument to the poet Abu Nawas (left); a young musician
playing a home-made instrument (right)*

literature adorn public places. The Baghdad Institute of Fine Arts
fosters the work of artists. In addition to the traditional Arabic
music and folk dancing, Baghdad has the Music and Ballet School
and the National Symphony Orchestra. Theater and film
production receives support. Poets and prose writers are valued.
The Iraqi poets, including a woman, Nazik al-Malaikah, were
among the pioneers of the use of free verse in Arabic.

All mass media are under government control. The major daily

*A bookshop in the courtyard of the Kadimain Mosque in Baghdad*

newspapers are in Arabic, and there are a variety of weekly and other periodicals published. English is the foreign language that is used most widely, but there are publications in other languages as well. Radio broadcasts are in several languages, and there are at least twenty television stations in the country. The government also supports the famous Iraqi Museum with its archaeological treasures; the National Museum of Modern Art with its permanent collection of Iraqi painting, sculpture, and ceramics; and the Museum of Iraqi Art Pioneers featuring the works of artists who developed the Iraqi modern art movement.

*A variety of clothing: children in contemporary clothing (left), a Kurdish girl wears typical bright colors (middle), and many Arab women still wear the traditional* abaya *(right).*

## WOMEN

The traditional *abaya*, which many Arab Iraqi women wear, is disappearing among educated women. This long cloak, which some think symbolizes women's seclusion, is justified as protecting the modesty of women and minimizing the importance of the money spent on clothes. The Kurdish women, although also Muslim, have traditionally dressed in bright-colored, though modest, clothing in contrast to the Arabs.

The status of women in Arab countries is not well understood in the West. In rural society and among less educated groups in cities, women live more sheltered lives. Their primary role is to care for the family and to raise children; work outside the home is rare. In traditional Arab society, women were very much under the control of their fathers or husbands and were valued in relationship to their ability to produce sons. But the status of women is changing as education spreads.

In Iraq, the National Action Charter that resulted from the revolution of 1971 states: "The liberation of woman from the feudalistic and bourgeois thinking and from the conditions and terms under which she was a sheer pleasure object or second-class citizen is a sacred hope and national duty for which one should struggle faithfully and keenly." The report of the 1963 Baath party Sixth National Conference states: "The emancipation of women is one of the major responsibilities of the national socialist revolution." Moreover, the party has organized a General Federation of Iraqi Women that plays a major role in implementing these ideals.

While Saddam Husain has given support to women, he also cautioned against simply adopting the Western ideas and practices. He faces the political problem of losing the backing of some of his supporters if he moves too quickly against some of the traditional practices of the culture.

What are the bright spots in the future for women? Many more women are being educated. More women, even of the lower classes, are employed in work for which they are paid. By the end of the war, women comprised 25 percent of the work force; and they occupied positions as lawyers, doctors, and engineers as well as teachers and welfare workers. Women have the right to vote and a number hold office, even as members of the national assembly. Many improvements have been made in family law as well. Women are expected to have greater leadership roles in Iraq's future, but change will have to come according to the planning of Iraqi women. It is evident that Iraqi women have come a long way since the days of the Ottoman Empire.

*Oil was discovered at Kirkuk in 1927. Fires from the burning of natural gas are called "eternal fires."*

# Chapter 7

# OIL AND FOOD

---

Until the discovery of oil in large quantities and the production of petroleum, agriculture was the most important part of the economy. It is still important, receiving 20 percent of the spending in the Socialist sector in the year 1981. The fact that Iraq has a larger population than some of its more sparsely settled neighbors provides the country with a potential for industrial development. The emphasis on education has helped to supply a work force with important skills.

Since the Baath party came to power in 1968, government control of the economy increased to the extent of 78 percent of Iraq's gross national product and 90 percent of imported goods. The private sector operations were concentrated in food processing, textiles, tourism, services, and retailing. However, in 1987 some of the state organizations for controlling the economy were abolished, and private companies were established. Since the cease-fire, Husain has announced the continuation of this trend.

Damage to the oil production facilities during the war and the military expenditures required by the war have been a setback to the growth the country had experienced prior to the hostilities. Many foreign companies have looked for ways of entering the market Iraq presents.

*Saudi Arabian delegates (center) at an OPEC meeting in 1976.*

## PETROLEUM

In 1980, before the war with Iran, Iraq was the second-largest supplier of crude oil. Only Saudi Arabia produced more. Iranian strikes knocked out key oil terminals. Refineries, pipelines, pumping stations, and petrochemical plants were damaged. Some refineries were in areas difficult to defend. Still new refineries were built in safer areas and old ones were being restored in 1989.

Also the pipelines that brought the oil to outside buyers were vulnerable. Iranian military action, guerrilla tactics attributed to the Kurds, and disputes with Syria over the line in its territory knocked out supply systems the Iraqis had used. New export pipelines were constructed across Turkey to the Mediterranean Sea and across Saudi Arabia to the Red Sea. These lines, and restoration of offshore gulf terminals, will increase Iraq's oil export capacity well beyond prewar levels.

Significant reserves of petroleum have been discovered. An

independent estimate of the proven published reserves of Iraq was 100,000 million barrels at the beginning of 1988—an amount sufficient to maintain production at current rates for many years.

It has been customary for 85 percent of the gas associated with the oil production to be burned. However, plans have been made to produce propane and butane and to feed gas into local industries. A petrochemical complex has been completed, which will produce polyethylene and caustic soda.

Iraq is one of the founding members of OPEC—the Organization of Petroleum Exporting Countries. While the country has opposed production cuts, it has argued for moderate prices. Iraq does not want to price itself out of the market. With petroleum accounting for 95 percent of the foreign exchange the country has earned, oil money is a key to Iraq's future plans.

## AGRICULTURE

Next to petroleum, agriculture is the most important sector of the economy. It employs 30 percent of the work force. Land reform in October 1958 required the redistribution of land if the holding exceeded 620 acres (251 hectares) on irrigated land or 1,240 acres (509 hectares) on land watered by rainfall. Agricultural cooperatives and state farms were established. However, agricultural productivity figures were disappointing. Now the government is willing to allow more private enterprise. State farms were abolished and companies and individuals are permitted to lease land at nominal rates.

Iraq grows a wide variety of crops. The most important are barley and wheat, but good rainfall is necessary for the best yields in these crops. Dates are the country's main export after

*Iraq is trying to increase its livestock industry (above). A farm family (above right), and a farmer harvesting barley (right)*

petroleum. Industrial uses for dates to produce sugar, alcohol, vinegar, and a protein concentrate have been found. Special banks have been established to help with loans for fish and poultry farms and animal husbandry projects.

The country wants to be self-sufficient in food supplies, but this goal would take a 25 percent increase in the land under cultivation. Iraq imports large quantities of apples, citrus fruits, eggs, frozen chicken, meat, and fish. The United States has been a major supplier of agricultural products, along with Canada and Australia. Efforts are being made to develop livestock and poultry farming in Iraq. Also there are plans to increase the fishing industry by improving freshwater fish resources. Iraq has plans for new agricultural colleges.

With proper placement of dams or reservoirs, the area of cultivated land in the country could be doubled. They also would provide some protection against disastrous floods and permit the

*A hydroelectric dam on the Tigris River*

creation of hydroelectric power. Iraq has a number of large dams
and reservoirs and several irrigation projects are underway.
Stagnant water is a problem because it adds to the salinity of the
soil.

## INDUSTRY

Before 1970 there were few large industries except for
petroleum. Around Baghdad there were some large operations
dealing with electricity and water supply and building materials.
Smaller industrial units were involved with date packing,
breweries, cigarettes, textiles, chemicals, furniture, shoes, jewelry,
and metalworking.

Recently, new industries have been built. An iron and steel
plant started production in 1978. Sulphur and phosphate rock are
being processed into sulphuric acid and phosphate fertilizer. A big

*Enlarging a canal for irrigation and drainage*

textile factory at Mosul is making calico from cotton. Sugar refineries, tractor assembly plants, paperboard factories, synthetic fiber manufacturing plants, and flour mills have been built. Cement works, brick production, and other factories for the construction industry have been started. The most recent projects include pharmaceuticals, electrical goods, telephone cables, and plastics. A great number of Eastern and Western bloc countries are involved in contracts for this industrial expansion.

Since electrical power stations were bombed by the Iranians, there has been activity to improve and extend the electrical networks. By 1985 the country's generating capacity was expected to provide electricity to almost all the rural areas. Moreover, the nation should benefit by being able to sell electricity to Turkey.

Iraq's experimental nuclear reactor was bombed by the Israeli air force in 1981. France, Saudi Arabia, Brazil, Portugal, Italy, and the Soviet Union all have been involved in assisting Iraq to establish a new reactor.

*A tug pulling strings of marsh boats*

## COMMUNICATION AND TRANSPORTATION

In the 1981-85 plan for Iraq, communication and transportation received special attention. A contract was awarded to British consultants to design an underground public transport system for Baghdad. Iraqi Airways bought several new planes from United States companies. French companies won the contract for the construction of a new Baghdad international airport. Other airports in the country are being expanded or planned.

Expansion of the facilities at the gulf port of Basra was halted by the Iran-Iraq War. The damage to that section of the country has been extensive, and it will take years to clean up the bombs and wreckage from the Shatt al-Arab River.

River transportation has been studied. Several stretches on the Tigris between Baghdad and Basra have been dredged. Navigation

*A motor launch used only by sheikhs*

potential studies have been ordered for the Euphrates between Haditha and al-Qurnah and even for the Tigris as a whole from Mosul to Basra. The latter project would be a large undertaking.

Expansion of the railway system was proposed with orders awarded to French, South Korean, and Brazilian firms. Also talks have been held with Kuwait, Saudi Arabia, and Turkey to link the Iraqi system with the rails of those countries in order to form a European-Gulf network.

Road construction has been encouraged. Major new highways, built during the war, link Iraq with Kuwait and Jordan. A new airport was opened in Basra after the war. Several other major road-building projects have been planned and the government is implementing a program for rural roads also.

Telecommunication systems have been modernized, including an earth satellite connection for international communications. It was expected that by 1985, ten out of every one hundred persons would own a private telephone.

# FINANCE AND TRADE

The difficulty in exporting large quantities of oil during the war years, the drop in oil prices, the heavy cost of the war with Iran, and the economic development plans have all been factors requiring Iraq to tap its reserves of foreign exchange. While specific information on these reserves is not available, some have estimated that the prewar figure of $35,000 million may have been wiped out completely. To try to control the deficits in the balance of payments, the government has tightly controlled foreign currency payments and imports.

Iraq has few banks and all are state controlled. The only commercial bank is Rafidain Bank established in 1941. It is the biggest Arab commercial bank, measured by deposits and gross assets. It has 228 local branches and 12 outside the country. Then there are 3 specialized banks for agricultural cooperatives, industrial operations, and real estate.

Most of Iraq's trade has been with Europe, the United States, Japan, and Turkey. France has been an important trading partner. Trade with the Soviet Union has been mostly for military supplies.

Until the war years, Iraq had not found it necessary to ask for loans from other countries. Revenues from petroleum supported the development plans and other needs the country had. Loans have been secured from other countries, from special Arab Funds, and from Euroloans (loans from European countries payable in a currency foreign to the debtor). Iraq's total foreign debt is estimated to be over $80,000 million. Some of this debt is loaned by Iraq's neighbors on the gulf and probably will not be repaid. However, money is needed each year for the portion of the debt owed to Western nations.

A panorama of Baghdad shows the
construction of new buildings (above),
men at a Baghdad sidewalk
café (below right), and the Baghdad
souk at dusk (below)

Baghdad

# Chapter 8

# A TOUR OF IRAQ

## BAGHDAD

Baghdad, the capital of the nation and the cultural center, has been described by some as the most exciting city of the Near East—better than Damascus in Syria or Cairo in Egypt. It is a modern city of many neighborhoods and districts. Its population reflects many ethnic groups that have made a home in this nation over the centuries. The recent economic boom has attracted Egyptian and Palestinian Arabs here.

The bazaar, or souk, is the area of many small shops. Here copper ware, that is hand beaten in the old traditional way to the accompaniment of much noise, is sold. The handwoven rug shops carry the Oriental carpets for which Iraq has been famous over the years. Beautiful gold and silver jewelry and the fragrance of coffee, tea, and spices are tempting.

Baghdad is home to eight great museums. There are shrines, mosques, schools, and palaces with beautiful architecture. Statues and monuments mark important events in Iraqi history. They add to the many parks that the citizens of Baghdad enjoy. Boat rides on the Tigris River are available. Restaurants and cafés are busy.

Scenes of Baghdad, considered by many to be one of the most cosmopolitan cities of the Near East.

*The Arch of Ctesiphon*

One of the dishes famous in Baghdad is the mazqouf fish that is cooked outdoors on wooden pegs placed around a fire of tamarisk wood. The fish is then spiced and served with pickles and vegetables.

Away from the gates and walls of the city are several historical sites. Tel Harmal, or Shadoboun, was an important site in Akkadian times. Tablets of law and mathematics have been found here. One tablet contains a geometrical solution of the theorem attributed to Euclid, composed some seventeen centuries before Euclid lived. Another ancient city to the northwest of Baghdad is Agargouf dating from the fifteenth century B.C. with the remains of a ziggurat. Over at al-Madain is the famous arch of Ctesiphon, from the Parthian Empire.

The National Theater in Baghdad seats one thousand and has a revolving stage with a fifty-foot (fifteen-meter) diameter. In the parks, Iraqi families play with their children in the cool night air of the Baghdad summer.

*Ruins at Babylon*

## EAST AND WEST OF BAGHDAD

The Diyala Province is to the east of the capital some forty-one miles (sixty-six kilometers) away. Its palm groves and citrus trees have been famous at least from the time of Arab historians of the past. Dating back six thousand years ago, this territory has produced many archaeological finds. Temples, palaces, clay tablets, and cylinder seals have been discovered as archaeologists have dug into the remains of cities of early civilizations.

West of Baghdad is al-Anbar Province that used to be called the Dulaim Liwa, after the tribes who lived there. Ar-Ramadi, the administrative center of this district, is about 65 miles (105 kilometers) from Baghdad. While ar-Ramadi is a comparatively new city, dating only from Ottoman times, many ancient cities have been found nearby. The old city of Hit is famous for its waterwheels on the Euphrates. It was an important source of bitumen in ancient times. Hadithah Dam on the Euphrates, important for irrigation and electricity, is located in this territory.

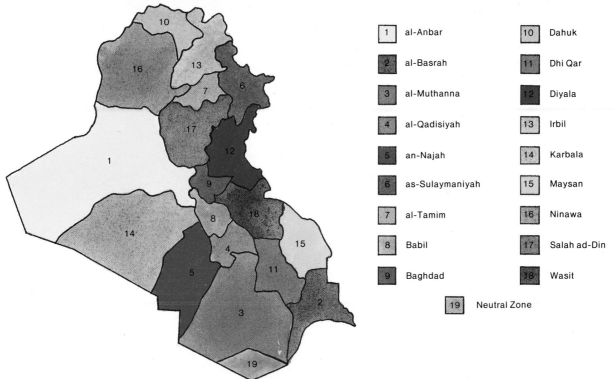

| | | | |
|---|---|---|---|
| 1 | al-Anbar | 10 | Dahuk |
| 2 | al-Basrah | 11 | Dhi Qar |
| 3 | al-Muthanna | 12 | Diyala |
| 4 | al-Qadisiyah | 13 | Irbil |
| 5 | an-Najah | 14 | Karbala |
| 6 | as-Sulaymaniyah | 15 | Maysan |
| 7 | al-Tamim | 16 | Ninawa |
| 8 | Babil | 17 | Salah ad-Din |
| 9 | Baghdad | 18 | Wasit |
| | | 19 | Neutral Zone |

Off the road to ar-Ramadi is the tourist village in Habbaniya, fifty-two miles (eighty-four kilometers) west of Baghdad. Here a six-story, air-conditioned hotel, conference hall, swimming pools, and recreational facilities form the largest tourist village of its kind in the Middle East. It is on one of the inland lakes.

## SOUTH OF BAGHDAD

The famous city of Babylon lies fifty-six miles (ninety kilometers) south of Baghdad. The current government is busy trying to reconstruct the ancient city. Babylon is an important symbol because it produced a great civilization that fought against both Israel and Persia (now Iran). Saddam Husain has been portrayed with Nebuchadrezzar as leaders who have brought Iraq to world recognition. At Babylon are the remains of the great Ishtar Gate and the Lion of Babylon. Nearby is a Greek theater from another era, which reminds people of Alexander the Great and his plans for the city as a capital of his empire.

*Left: A shopping arcade in Karbala   Right: Beautiful mosaic work decorates the entrance to a mosque in the holy city of Karbala.*

Not far away is al-Uhaimir, the ancient city of Kish. Here is the city of the Akkadian King Sargon, who transformed the city-states into an empire.

Karbala and Najaf are cities that are sacred to the Shiites as pilgrim cities. Ali, son-in-law of Muhammad, after he had been stabbed in A.D. 661, asked that he be placed on a camel and that he be buried wherever the camel knelt. That place was Najaf. It is the site of the beautiful shrine to which thousands of pilgrims come each year. It is also home to famous religious universities and schools. Ali's two sons, Husain and Abbas, are buried in separate shrines in Karbala. These cities are on the edge of the desert that stretches to the west. Other famous Arab sites are the Ukhaidhir Castle that dates to the beginning of the Abbasid period; Ain

Left: Part of the eighty-foot wall
that enclosed the palace in Nippur
Right: The golden domes of mosques
and minarets can be seen from the
center of Karbala.

al-Tamr, which is an oasis on the western plateau that figured in
the Arab conquest of the territory; and Kufa, which was founded
in A.D. as the first Arab capital.

Dating back to earlier civilizations are the archaeological sites at
Nippur, 112 miles (180 kilometers) southwest of Baghdad, and
Uruk, near Warka, that have provided the remarkable finds
introducing historians to the Sumerian civilization. This was the
home of King Gilgamesh, perhaps the one after whom the epic
was fashioned. It was from the tombs of Ur that the beautiful
helmets, crowns, and harps came that showed how great a
civilization had existed here in 2450 B.C. There may be many more
important sites that will reveal even more about the beginning of
civilization.

*Marsh Arabs make their homes of reeds, which they gather and dry.*

The marshes provide a huge expanse of water dotted with islands of reeds and mud. The multitude of fish, birds, and game that inhabit this area have made it attractive to humans who have lived in huts of reeds with elaborate designs. Boats are the way to get around to the island. Fish are caught with nets or speared with a five-pronged instrument called a *fala*. It is thought that the marshes formed before Sumerian times as the gulf waters receded leaving the marshes along the Tigris and Euphrates. Whether this way of life will survive the war that was concentrated in this area, and the industrialization and water projects, only the future will tell.

Basra is the port city on the gulf from which Sindbad the Sailor of Sheherazade's story began his journey. The city is 341 miles (549 kilometers) from Baghdad and 42 miles (67 kilometers) north of the gulf. It was founded on orders from Caliph Umar ibn al-Khattab in A.D. 637 and has been a major city with great mosques and libraries. Famous philosophers and scientists have

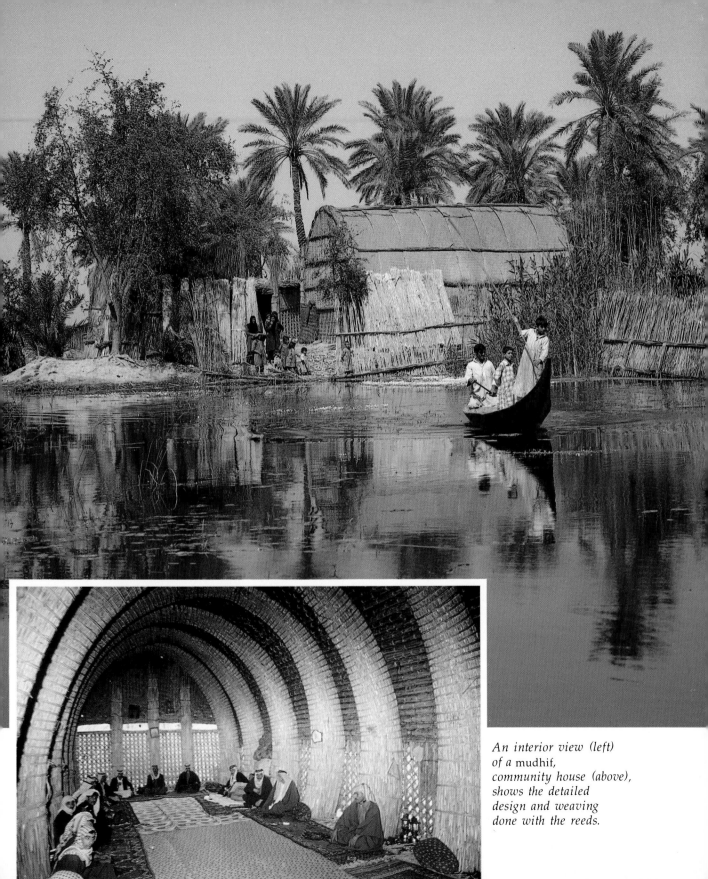

An interior view (left)
of a mudhif,
community house (above),
shows the detailed
design and weaving
done with the reeds.

*Left: The al-Malwiyah minaret in Samarra*
*Right: A panorama of Mosul*

come from this city. Unfortunately, Basra was heavily shelled during the war by the Iranians but Iraq has reconstructed much of it.

## NORTH FROM BAGHDAD

Samarra was briefly the capital of the Abbasid Empire. The spiral minaret of the great mosque is famous. It is 171-feet (52-meters) high. Palaces and shrines also are found in this city.

Farther north in the territory that was the stronghold of the Assyrians is the large city of Mosul. This city is a center for trade, industry, communication, and education. The spring festival of Mosul is noted for flower processions and folk dancing. The city has a number of old mosques. One has a minaret that is bent and has elaborate brickwork designs. There is a mosque of the prophet Jonah, for Nineveh, the city that Jonah was sent to warn, is close

110

*Near Nimrud, these women are making sun-dried bricks, using the same methods as their ancestors.*

by. Also there are old Christian churches and monasteries, one dating back to the fourth century A.D. Here one will see ruins of ancient castles and city walls. A museum houses archaeological finds of the area. The city is the beginning of roads leading into the northern resort areas. One can stay in chalets near forests and waterfalls.

Nineveh and Nimrud, capital of the Assyrian Empire, are being protected and reconstructed in places. Some of the beautiful bas-reliefs are still in place, although most of them were removed by foreign excavators before there were any limits on their removal. Khorsabad and Assur also are sites of former capitals of the Assyrian Empire.

Al-Hadr, fifty miles (eighty kilometers) south of Mosul, was one of the great caravan cities in the second and third centuries A.D. Impressive ruins remain of temples where the sun god, the eagle, Venus, and the god, Nergoul, who was symbolized by the planet Mars, were worshiped.

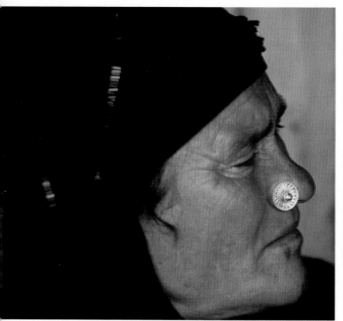 

The Dahuk Region lies forty-five miles (seventy-three kilometers) from Mosul. It is famous for its grapes, figs, and pomegranates. A famous Abbasid stone bridge shows the engineering skills of another era. In this cooler hill country with forests and waterfalls, there are a number of summer resorts.

As-Sulaymaniyah Region is known for its woods and forests—especially walnut trees. Some of the oldest settlements dating back to paleolithic times are found here. The Akkadians and the Assyrians also ruled the territory. Here the Kurdish culture is strong.

The Irbil Region also provides resorts with the scenic beauty of mountaintops and the shade of poplars and cypresses. Walnuts, almonds, pomegranates, grapes, apples, and pears come from this area. The plain of Harai Batass is fertile and famous for honey and tobacco. In this district near Ruwanduz is the Shanidar Cave in which the skeletons of the Neanderthals were found. In winter, the temperature can drop to five degrees Fahrenheit (minus fifteen

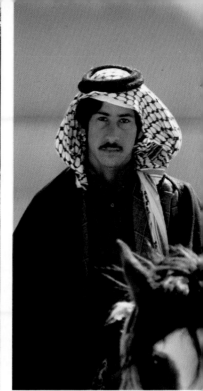

degrees Celsius). With snow, skiers are attracted to the resorts.

Finally, there is al-Tamim Province. Here in Jarmo, we have evidence that humans learned to plant seeds rather than just gather food. Traces of the Sumerians and the Akkadians have been found in cuneiform inscriptions. The oldest map in the world, dating back 4,300 years to the Akkadian Empire, has been found in this district.

## THE HISTORY OF HUMANKIND

A trip around Iraq is a trip through the history of humankind. The civilizations that existed in this territory have enriched those that followed. Now Iraq is developing her industrial base with money from petroleum and her human potential with education. Her long war against Iran, the land of one of her traditional enemies, and her attempt to annex Kuwait are evidence that Iraq is attempting to claim a leadership role among her Arab neighbors.

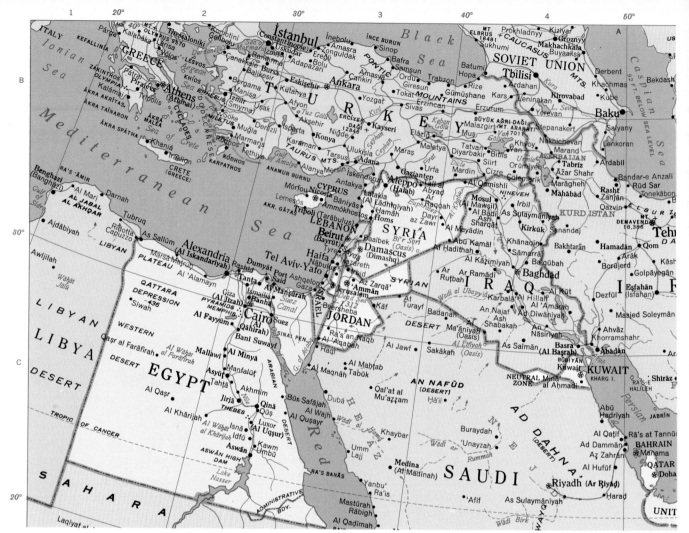

**MAP KEY**

| | | | |
|---|---|---|---|
| Ad Diwaniyah | B4 | Ash Sharqat | B4 |
| Al Amarah | B4 | Baqubah | B4 |
| Al Badi | B4 | Baghdad | B4 |
| Al Haditha (Al Hadithah) | B4 | Basra (Al Basrah) | B4 |
| Al Hillah | B4 | Irbil | B4 |
| Al Kazimiyah | B4 | Karbala | B4 |
| Al Kut | B4 | Khanaqin | B4 |
| An Nasiriyah | B4 | Kirkuk | B4 |
| An Najaf | B4 | Mosul (Al Mawsil) | B4 |
| Ar Ramadi | B4 | Nineveh (historic ruins) | B4 |
| Ar Rutbah | B4 | Samarra | B4 |
| As Salman | B4 | Shatt al-Arab (river) | B4, C4 |
| As Sulaymaniyah | B4 | Tigris (river) | B4 |
| Ash Shabakah | B4 | Wadi al Ubayyid (river or stream) | B4 |

# MINI-FACTS AT A GLANCE

## GENERAL INFORMATION

**Official Name:** Republic of Iraq

**Capital:** Baghdad

**Official Languages:** Arabic and Kurdish. Kurdish is spoken in Kurdistan.

**Government:** Iraq is a one-party state governed by the Arab Baath Socialist party. The Revolutionary Command Council (RCC) exacts legislation by decree.

The nominal legislature is the 250-member National Assembly, a bicameral body. The highest judicial authority is the Court of Cassation. Each of the religious communities has its own religious court that considers question of personal status, marriage, and inheritance.

There are eighteen provinces.

**Religion:** Muslims make up about 95 percent of the population. While more than 50 percent of Muslims are Shiites, the leaders of the party in power since 1968 are mostly Sunnis. There is a very small Jewish population.

**Flag:** The national flag is a tricolor of red, white, and black horizontal stripes, with three five-pointed stars in green in the center of the white stripe. The flag was adopted in 1963.

**National Anthem:** "Al-Salaam al-Jumhuri" ("Salute of the Republic")

**Money:** The Iraqi dinar (ID) is a paper currency of 1,000 fils. In 1990 1 ID equaled $3.216 in U.S. currency.

**Weights and Measures:** The metric system is the legal standard, but weights and measures in general use vary, especially in domestic transactions. The unit of land is the dunam, which is equivalent to .62 acres (.25 hectares).

**Population:** Approximately 17,754,000 (mid-1991 estimate); 71.6 percent urban, 28.4 rural

**Major Cities:**

Baghdad . . . . . . . . . . . . . . . . . . . . . . . . . . . . . . . . . . . . . . . . . . . . . . . 4,648,609
Basra . . . . . . . . . . . . . . . . . . . . . . . . . . . . . . . . . . . . . . . . . . . . . . . . 616,700
Mosul . . . . . . . . . . . . . . . . . . . . . . . . . . . . . . . . . . . . . . . . . . . . . . . . 570,926
Kirkuk . . . . . . . . . . . . . . . . . . . . . . . . . . . . . . . . . . . . . . . . . . . . . . . 207,852

(Population based on mid-1991 estimate.)

# GEOGRAPHY

**Highest Point:** Mount Halgurd, 12,230 ft. (3,728 m)

**Lowest Point:** Sea level

**Rivers:** The Tigris and Euphrates join at al-Qurnah to become the Shatt al-Arab for the final 115 mi. (185 km) to the Persian Gulf. The rivers flood in the lower sections and have swift currents in the upper sections. Transportation is difficult.

**Mountains:** Iraq is mainly comprised of lowlands. Less than 15 percent of the country rises above 5,000 ft. (1,524 m). The northeastern mountain region, Iraqi Kurdistan, is part of the Zagros Mountain system.

**Climate:** The intensely hot and dry summers last from May to October, and during the hottest part of the day—often 120° F. (49° C) in the shade—people seek refuge in underground shelters. Winters last from December to March. They are damp and relatively cold—averaging 50° F. (10° C). Spring and fall are periods of transition. Annual rainfall is less than 15 in. (38 cm).

The climate of the Tigris-Euphrates Basin is overwhelmingly hot in summer and humid near the rivers. Sandstorms are frequent during the summer months.

There are two types of wind: the *sharqi*, a dry, gusty wind from the south or southeast, and the *shamal*, very dry air from the north and northwest that prevails from mid-June to mid-September.

**Greatest Distances:** North to south: 530 mi. (853 km)
East to west: 495 mi. (797 km)

**Area:** 169,235 sq. mi. (438,317 km²)

# NATURE

**Trees:** Willow, poplar, and alder trees are prevalent in the lower regions of the Tigris and Euphrates. In the higher Zagros Mountains the valonia oak, the bark of which is used for tanning leather, is grown. Date palms are prevalent and produce a major export.

**Animals:** Wild animals include the jackal, hyena, fox, gazelle, antelope, mole, porcupine, bat, and desert hare.

**Birds:** There are many game birds: wild ducks, geese, and partridge. Falcons are trained for hunting.

# EVERYDAY LIFE

**Housing:** In older sections of Iraq today, mud-and-brick houses are plastered and whitewashed and built around an inside courtyard. Modern Iraqi houses have high-walled roofs that afford privacy for warm-weather sleeping in the out-of-doors.

**Holidays:**

> January 1, New Year's Day
> January 6, Army Day
> February 8, Fourteenth Ramadan Revolution Day
> May 1, Labor Day
> July 14, Declaration of the Republic
> July 17, Peaceful Revolution Day

**Culture:** The rich cultural life of Iraq has been largely Arab. The ancient traditions in architecture, sculpture, painting, weaving, and carpet making are flourishing today.

Poetry and prose literature are of particular interest. Poetry is a popular art, and it is not confined to the educated or the wealthy. Nazik al-Malaikah, a woman, is an important contemporary poet. The most famous piece of Sumerian literature is the *Epic of Gilgamesh.*

Most of the plays produced in Iraq are sociopolitical in content. European works also are performed regularly. Attempts by the government to revive folk music and dance have met with some success. Music sung in colloquial Arabic is the most popular.

Important painters and sculptors include Khaled ar-Rahhal, Jawad Salim, Akram Shukri, and Hafidh ad-Durubi.

The National Museum and the Museum of Arab Antiquities in Baghdad house the country's archaeological heritage. The Baghdad Institute of Fine Arts, the National Museum of Modern Art, the Museum of Iraqi Art Pioneers, the Music and Ballet School, and the National Symphony Orchestra enhance cultural life.

There are many cinemas in Baghdad, and Egyptian, Indian, American, Italian, and Russian films are popular. Theater and film production receives support.

**Sports and Recreation:** Soccer is the national game. It is far more popular than basketball, volleyball, swimming, and boxing.

**Transportation:** The railways are state owned. Nearly half of the roads are unpaved, but road construction is being encouraged.

There are 631 mi. (1,015 km) of inland waterways, 65 mi. (105 km) of which are navigable by seagoing ships. The principal ports are Basra and Umm Qasr. Baghdad and Basra have international airports, and Mosul has a domestic airport. Iraqi Airlines is state owned and provides national and international service.

**Communication:** The press is controlled by the government. It is supposed to promote the view of the Arab Baath Socialist party. The major daily newspapers are in Arabic, but there are publications in other languages as well. The radio and television network is state run. Fourteen radio stations and thirteen TV stations are in operation. Broadcasts are in several languages. Telecommunications systems have been modernized.

**Education:** Stamping out illiteracy has been one of the goals of the government since the revolution in 1968. Primary and secondary education are free. The six-year secondary-education program consists of intermediate-secondary and intermediate-preparatory levels. In 1981 it was estimated that 49 percent of the appropriate age group were in secondary schools.

There are 46 teacher-training institutes, 19 technical institutes, and 6 universities.

**Health and Welfare:** Increasing commitment to Socialist policies has resulted in an expansion of welfare services, including health facilities and housing projects for the poor, especially in Baghdad, and benefits for old age, unemployment, maternity, marriage, death, and sickness.

There are some health problems. Poor sanitary conditions and polluted and stagnant water spread diseases in some areas. Infant mortality is high. Trained medical personnel are in very short supply. Expansion of health facilities was a priority under the 1981-85 five-year plan. Thirty new hospitals were built. Life expectancy is low—65 years for men and 67 years for women.

## ECONOMY AND INDUSTRY

**Principal Products:**
*Agriculture:* Grapes, dates, watermelons, tomatoes, beans, rice, barley, wheat, cotton
*Mining:* Petroleum, sulfur, gypsum, salt, phosphates
*Manufacturing:* Refined petroleum products, iron and crude steel, nitrogenous fertilizers, cement, raw sugar, cotton and woolen textiles, carpets

## IMPORTANT DATES

120,000 B.C.—Axes and scrapers dating from this period have been found in northern Iraq

3500-300 B.C.—Sumerians gather together in cities along the delta region of the Tigris and the Euphrates rivers

2350 B.C.—Sumerian city-states are formed into an empire under Akkadian leader Sargon

c. 2400-2200 B.C.—Akkadian civilization flourishes

2000 B.C.—Elamites attack and destroy Ur

1800 B.C.—Babylonian Empire is formed

935 B.C.—Rise of the new Assyrian Empire

612 B.C.—Assyrian Empire suddenly collapses; beginning of Chaldean or neo-Babylonian civilization

539 B.C.—Achaemenian or Persian period begins

330 B.C.—Alexander the Great conquers the Persians and attempts to restore the city of Babylon

A.D. 637—Arabs conquer the Persians

750-1258—Abbasid family rules

762—Baghdad founded as capital of Abbasid Empire

1055—Toghril Beg conquers Baghdad

1258—Hulagu, grandson of Genghis Khan, conquers Baghdad

1401—Mongols again capture Baghdad

1530—Ottomans (Turks), led by Sulayman the Magnificent, conquer Baghdad and hold land until 1918

Mid-17th to 19th centuries—European trading in the Persian Gulf area expands

1914-18—World War I—Britain occupies Iraq

1920—Great Britain is invited by the League of Nations to serve as the mandatory power for Iraq; temporary Arab government is established—to be assisted by British advisers and answerable to British high commissioner for Iraq

1921—Prince Faisal is crowned King Faisal I

1923—Oil is discovered at Kirkuk

1924—Sheikh Mahmud, a Kurdish tribal leader, is expelled by the British after intrigues with Turkish tribes on the frontier

1925—Constitution provides for bicameral legislature, limiting powers of the monarchy

1932—British mandate ends; Iraq is recognized as a sovereign and independent state

1933—King Faisal I dies; his son Ghazi succeeds to throne

1939—Ghazi dies, is succeeded by Faisal II

1941—British occupy Iraq

1943—Iraq declares war on Axis powers

1945—Iraq's prime minister plays important role in establishment of Arab League

1948—Uprising against proposed Portsmouth Treaty with Britain

1952—Agreement with Iraq Petroleum Co. brings Iraq increase in oil royalties; Iraq joins Arab League Collective Security Pact

1954—Iraq accepts United States offer of military aid

1955 — Baghdad Pact joins Iraq, Britain, Pakistan, and Iran in a pro-Western, anti-Communist security pact, opposed by Egypt

1958 — United Arab Republic (Egypt and Syria) is formed; Iraq and Jordan form their own federation; King Faisal II is killed in a coup: Brigadier-General Abd al-Karim Qasim becomes prime minister; Iraq severs its pact with Jordan; Iraq restores diplomatic relations with the U.S.S.R.

1959 — Iraq withdraws from the Baghdad Pact

1963 — Qasim is overthrown by the Baath party; the Baath party is subsequently ousted and Abd as-Salem Arif is appointed president

1966 — Arif is killed in a helicopter accident and his brother, General Abd ar-Rahman Arif, becomes president

1968 — Arif is overthrown and replaced by a junta headed by Ahmad Hasan al-Bakr, head of the Baath party

1971 — Iraq and the Soviet Union conclude a 15-year treaty of friendship

1972 — Iraq nationalizes the petroleum industry, forming Iraq Petroleum Company (IPC)

1975 — Algiers Agreement settles border with Iran

1978 — Al-Bakr resigns and is succeeded by Saddam Husain

1980 — Iraq invades Iran; Iran-Iraq War begins

1981 — Israel bombs a French-supplied Iraqi nuclear reactor

1984 — Iraq resumes diplomatic relations with the United States

1988 — Cease-fire in the Iran-Iraq War

1990 — Iraq invades Kuwait and annexes it; United States and international troops sent to Saudi Arabia to help restore Kuwait's sovereignty; United Nations Security Council condemns Iraq's action against Kuwait and imposes an embargo on goods entering Iraq

1991 — In operation "Desert Storm" multinational allied forces bomb Iraq and retake Kuwait, driving out the Iraqi forces

1992 — Since the weapons inventory did not include nuclear materials as required, the 1990 embargo remains in effect. Saddam Husain remains in power

# IMPORTANT PEOPLE

Abd al-Ilah (1913-58), regent and crown prince to Faisal II, 1939; gave throne to Faisal II in 1953

Aishah (611-78), Muhammad's widow; daughter of Abu Bakr

Ali, Muhammad's cousin and son-in-law; reigned as caliph from 656 to 661

Abd ar-Rahman Arif (1916-    ), brother of Abd as-Salam Arif; president from 1966 to 1968

Abd as-Salam Arif (1921-1966), army officer; leader of revolutionary coup in 1958; became president in 1966

Ashurnasirpal II, reigned from 883 to 859 B.C.; created new Assyrian Empire, built huge palace at Nimrud and made Nimrud the capital

Abu Bakr, successor to Muhammad; reigned from 632 to 634

Ahmad Hasan al-Bakr (1914-1979), Brigidier general; president from 1968 to 1979

Adud al-Dawlah, member of Buyid family; Shiite ruler from 944 to 983; reign noted for public works

Eannatum of Lagash, king about 2460 B.C.; claimed dominion over Sumer

Faisal I (1885-1933), first king of Iraq, ruled from 1921 to 1933; negotiated treaties with Britain, including 1930 treaty that gave independence to Iraq

Faisal II (1935-58), became king in 1939 at age of four, came to power in 1953; was executed during an overthrow of the monarchy

Fatimah (c. 616-33), first daughter of Muhammad; wife of Ali

Rashid Ali al-Gailani (1892-1964), pro-German leader during 1930s and 1940s

Ghazi (1912-39), son of Faisal I, king of Iraq from 1933 to 1939

Gudea, erected fifteen temples in the city of Girsum about 2350 B.C., during the reign of Ur-Nammu

Hammurabi, ruler of Babylonian Empire from 1792 to 1750 B.C.; developed legal code

Hulagu, grandson of Genghis Khan who ruled from 1217 to 1265; conquered Baghdad in 1258 and overthrew Abbasid Empire

Husain (c. 629-80), second son of Ali, grandson of Muhammad

Saddam Husain (1937-    ), present-day ruler of Iraq; became president in 1979

Umar ibn al-Khattab, companion of Muhammad; waged *jihad*, holy war, against unbelievers; reigned from 634 to 644

Nazik al-Malaikah (1923-    ), comtemporary female poet

Muawiyah, cousin of Uthman; ruler of Damascus from 661 to 680

Muhammad (570-632), prophet and founder of Islam

Nebuchadrezzar I (c. 1124-1103 B.C.), king; attacked and conquered Elam and Assyria; ruled most of Mesopotamia

Nebuchadrezzar II (c. 630-562 B.C.), defeated Egyptians; restored Babylon and other cities; king of Babylon from 605 to 562 B.C.

Abd al-Karim Qasim (1914-1963), head of revolutionary forces that overthrew King Faisal II in 1958

Harun al-Rashid, Caliph in Baghdad from 786 to 809

Rimush, son of Sargon, reigned from 2315 to 2307 B.C. over the territory his father conquered

Abu al-Abbas as-Saffah, founder of Abbasid Empire that ruled from 750 to 1258; reigned from 750 to 754

Nuri as-Said (1888-1958), pro-British leader during the 1930s and 1940s

Sammuramat, mother of King Adad-nirari III, queen regent of Assyria from 784 to 780 B.C.

Sargon the Great, king of the Akkadians; ruled Mesopotamia from about 2371 to 2316 B.C.

Sargon II, king from 721 to 705 B.C.; widened the Assyrian Empire to the Mediterranean Sea and the Persian Gulf

Sennacherib (705-681 B.C.), attacked Judah and laid siege to Jerusalem; active in restoring Nineveh to great splendor

Shalmaneser III, son of Ashurnasirpal II; reigned over Assyrian Empire from 858 to 825 B.C.

Shulgi, son of Ur-Nammu; second king of Sumerian Dynasty from 2095 to 2048 B.C.; consolidated empire; built many temples, some of which exist today

Naram-Sin, son of Manishtusu; fourth king of Akkadian Dynasty founded by Sargon, from 2291 to 2255 B.C.

Sulayman the Magnificent, great Ottoman (Turkish) leader who ruled from 1520 to 1566; added Baghdad to his territories; encouraged arts and sciences

Sulayman II (1641-91), faced disturbed conditions within Turkey; carried on an unsuccessful war with Austria

Tamerlane (1336-1405), Eastern conqueror; Mongol leader; conquered Baghdad in 1393

Tiglathpileser I, king of Assyria from about 1115 to 1077 B.C.; extended Assyrian dominions; renowned as mighty hunter

Tiglathpileser III, king of Assyria from 745 to 727 B.C.; one of the most powerful leaders in the Assyrian Empire

Toghril Beg (c. 990-1063), Sunni ruler; conquered Baghdad in 1055

Ur-Nammu, ruled from 2112 to 2095 B.C.; during his reign the oldest collection of laws was developed

Uthman, founder of Umayyad Dynasty, reigned from 664 to 656

# INDEX

Page numbers that appear in boldface type indicate illustrations

## About the Author

Leila Merrell Foster is a lawyer, United Methodist minister, and clinical psychologist with degrees from Northwestern University and Garrett Evangelical Theological Seminary. She is the author of books and articles on a variety of subjects.

Dr. Foster's love of travel began early as she listened to her mother and older sister read aloud travel and adventure stories. As a youngster, she enjoyed the family trips through which she learned geography, geology, history, art, agriculture, and economics in a very pleasant manner.

Dr. Foster also has written Enchantment of the World: *Bhutan*.